Praise for I Didn't Come Here to Lie

"Karen Lewis changed the world. Her legacy lives on in the work of countless organizers committed to transforming the lives of young people, and this book is a welcome assurance that her lessons endure for generations to come." —EVE L. EWING, author of *Ghosts in the Schoolyard: Racism and School Closings on Chicago's South Side*

"Karen Lewis's story, as captured in this book, is remarkable and deeply inspiring. It's a narrative of resilience, resistance, and the relentless pursuit of justice that will galvanize readers to imagine and work toward a more equitable future. Thank you, Karen Lewis, for leaving us with a road map for freedom dreams—a gift that will inspire generations to come." —BETTINA LOVE, author of *Punished for Dreaming: How School Reform Harms Black Children and How We Heal*

"Karen Lewis was one of Chicago's most powerful labor and community leaders and was as humble and generous as she was fierce and formidable. We need more like her. I admired her greatly, and her legacy offers important lessons for this generation of labor, left, and antiracist organizers. Who better to help share her story than the amazing Chicago educator and historian Elizabeth Todd-Breland? *I Didn't Come Here to Lie* is a must-read in order to prepare us for all the truth-telling that must happen if we are to survive and advance in these dangerous but dynamic political times." —BARBARA RANSBY, historian, activist, and author of *Ella Baker and the Black Freedom Movement*

"*I Didn't Come Here to Lie* is a memoir as fearless, insightful, hilarious, and fiercely honest as Karen herself. This book offers unique insight into the sharp humor and brilliant wit that defined Karen—qualities that made her not just a formidable labor leader but also a beloved friend and mentor. It doesn't just tell Karen's story; it inspires us to laugh, resist, and work together for a better world. *I Didn't Come Here to Lie* serves as a blueprint for collective action in the pursuit of social justice and will endure as a lasting inspiration for changemakers for generations to come." —**JESSE HAGOPIAN**, author of *Teach Truth: The Struggle for Antiracist Education*

I Didn't Come Here to Lie

My Life and Education

Karen G.J. Lewis, NBCT

Elizabeth Todd-Breland

Haymarket Books
Chicago, Illinois

Published in 2025 by
Haymarket Books
P.O. Box 180165
Chicago, IL 60618
www.haymarketbooks.org

ISBN: 979-8-88890-253-0

Distributed to the trade in the US through Consortium Book Sales and Distribution (www.cbsd.com) and internationally through Ingram Publisher Services International (www.ingramcontent.com).

This book was published with the generous support of Lannan Foundation, Wallace Action Fund, and Marguerite Casey Foundation.

Cover and interior design by Eric Kerl.
Cover photo: Karen Lewis addresses the crowd during a rally in Chicago. (AP Photo/Charles Rex Arbogast).

Library of Congress Cataloging-in-Publication data is available.

10 9 8 7 6 5 4 3 2 1
Printed in Canada

Contents

Foreword

Angela Y. Davis

I was not paying much attention to the news until an imposing Black woman on the television screen began to confront Mayor Rahm Emanuel with the kind of confidence and eloquence that would arrest anyone's attention. It was 2012, and the Chicago Teachers Union had gone on strike with Karen Lewis as the president of the union. Over the course of the strike, people all over the country learned about the concerted attack on education in Chicago and elsewhere, especially when it came to students of color and the schools in their communities. We learned especially about the ravages of privatization and the effort underway to offer up our public schools to the altar of profit.

I first saw Karen Lewis in person in 2014 at a conference in Chicago, organized by Barbara Ransby under the rubric "Freedom Dreams," the title of Robin D. G. Kelly's brilliant exploration of the Black radical imagination. Barbara, Robin, and I, as well as so many others in attendance at the conference, joined the effort to persuade her to run against Rahm Emanuel in the upcoming mayoral election. We told her we were committed to making this the most exciting mayoral campaign in Chicago since Harold Washington's 1983 victory, and we talked about the national and international implications her run for mayor was certain to develop. As she explains in this extraordinary memoir, her health crisis caused her to forego this freedom dream. But even as she bequeathed this struggle to someone who might take it up in the future, she began to work on another freedom dream—her own story. The very last time I saw Karen, she was deeply ensconced in the work on her memoir, which will certainly inspire more freedom dreams for many years to come.

Reading her captivating memoir, *I Didn't Come Here to Lie,* made me realize why I have always felt so moved by Karen's contributions and how deeply I will always appreciate her legacy. I also realized how much I have in common with her. Like Karen, I am a teacher who comes from a family of educators: both our mothers and fathers were dedicated teachers. And, like Karen, I believe that working people and their unions always deserve our vigorous support. Karen Lewis is clearly one of the most compelling labor leaders of our time, and I would position her in those two related and intersecting traditions. Actually, now that I am considering the traditions of Black woman educators and labor leaders, I can also think of other associated traditions that include, for example, revolutionary activists, and antiracist, anticapitalist feminists, with which she also is aligned. But for the moment I want to focus on educators and unionists.

I see Karen Lewis as coming from a long line of teachers who participated in and were at the very heart of the struggle for Black liberation. Like Susie King Taylor, Charlotte Forten, and Ida B. Wells, for example, they have always known that there can be no liberation without education. These women taught the children and adults of their communities—even, as was the case for Susie King Taylor, when it was a punishable crime to teach and learn reading and writing. Today, in this era of global capitalism, the devastating carcerality associated with the rise of the prison-industrial complex and its juggernaut of privatization turns public schools into places where discipline is valued over learning. Students move seamlessly from sites of putative education to sites of incarceration. Karen was determined to reinvigorate public education so that students might discover their passions and embark on journeys toward better futures. She remains a shining light, an inspiration to all those who want to reconnect with the emancipatory tradition of public education.

As an activist who learned very early in my life to respect the value and power of the labor movement, I often boast about the fact that in my eight decades on this planet I have never once crossed a picket line. In 1981, I drove from Vancouver to Oakland in order to avoid violating the air traffic controllers strike, which, unfortunately, was broken by the Reagan administration. I am still saddened by the fact that I never got to tell Karen about one of the truly proud moments of my life, when I was inducted as an honorary member into the International Longshore and Warehouse Union, Local 10. Radical union leaders, especially Black women, have always been the movement people with whom I have emphatically identified. Thanks to the phenomenal work of Karen Lewis, one day people will also be aware of Black women union leaders like Dora Lee Jones, who helped to found the Domestic Workers Union in Harlem during the 1930s, and Moranda Smith, a pivotal organizer of the Tobacco Workers Union in North Carolina during the 1940s, who in 1947 became the first Black woman to join the executive leadership of an international union, the Food, Tobacco, Agricultural, and Allied Workers Union. Moranda Smith was also a member of the Communist Party.

Those of us who knew Karen Lewis or followed her public interventions will always notice a void, especially in community conversations about public education. But her voice has also helped to advance discussions about racism, labor struggles, feminism, and politics more broadly. After reading the section of her memoir in which she writes about her spirituality and her decision to convert to Judaism, I found myself wishing that she were still able to contribute to current conversations regarding the Israeli war on Gaza and ongoing genocidal attacks on Palestinians who live in the West Bank and inside the territory Israel has claimed since 1948. As she insists in these pages, she is a devout Jew, who has learned to read and pronounce Hebrew, who has taken classes on Hebrew and Jewish culture, and who has struggled in many ways around her chosen religion. Since she makes it very clear that she does not support Israel and its apartheid practices, I think she would be very proud of the progressive Jewish activists who are leading the campaign to force the US government, the most important among Israel's allies, to cease providing funds and military aid to the state of Israel.

¡Karen Lewis, presenté!

Preface

A Note on Process

Jill Petty and Elizabeth Todd-Breland

Completing Karen's memoir posthumously has been a tremendous honor and an amazing gift. From the beginning of the project, we felt a great responsibility to make certain that Karen's wishes for this book came to fruition. But after Karen passed in 2021, this project felt even more urgent. It was a team effort, with Elizabeth as coauthor, Jill as editor, and others supporting along the way. Above all, Karen's husband, John Lewis, supported and encouraged us throughout. We are so grateful that Karen entrusted us with bringing her passion project, this memoir, to life. The following is a note on process and method.

When Jill secured an in-person appointment to meet Chicago Teachers Union (CTU) president Karen Lewis for the first time, she was over the moon. Jill was a veteran editor, working at Beacon Press at the time. She had met with many prominent people during her more than fifteen years in publishing, but this was different. Jill is the kid of a longtime Chicago Public Schools

(CPS) teacher who was also a proud CTU member, so arranging to meet "Madam President" felt akin to meeting royalty. She was going to see the "People's Queen!"

Indeed, by the summer of 2016, when Jill scheduled the meeting, Karen was absolutely beloved in Chicago (particularly among Black Chicagoans) for her forthrightness, fearlessness, and fierce determination to get the very best for Chicago's then 380,000 public school students. Karen was exceptionally astute, passionate, and unapologetically progressive: a force to be reckoned with. A living legend.

When Jill and Karen connected for the first time, Karen was two years removed from surgery for a cancerous brain tumor and was back at the helm of the CTU. They met to discuss Karen writing an introduction for a book that Jill was editing. In the following weeks, as they worked together on her introduction, Jill asked Karen if she'd ever considered writing a memoir. Karen admitted that she had thought about it. She knew that she was a hell of a storyteller, and while she didn't necessarily have enough time to write the book, she knew she had the goods. After all, over the course of her life, Karen Lewis had broken many of the rules Black women are supposed to follow; instead, she resolutely bucked conventions, shattered barriers, and embraced her own wisdom and idiosyncrasies.

As Jill and Karen talked more about Karen's own narrative, they started to imagine and sketch the first couple of chapters of her memoir. A lifelong learner and seeker, Karen said her goal was to humanize—not lionize—herself. She wanted this book to reduce (not increase) any artificial distance between her and her readers. So, with the working title *My Best Decisions*, Jill and Karen discussed how to move forward with writing the memoir. They also realized that, given Karen's towering responsibilities and always-jammed schedule, her memoir project desperately needed another set of hands.

Around this time, in March 2017, Elizabeth interviewed Karen for her own book project, *A Political Education: Black Politics and Education Reform in Chicago Since the 1960s*, which was published by University of North Carolina Press in 2018. Elizabeth had been spending a lot of time at CTU headquarters conducting historical research with old copies of the *Chicago Union Teacher* newsletter. She gave a lunch talk on this work in progress for CTU staff that Karen attended. At the talk, Karen shared amazing stories of her youth activism and connected her personal experiences as an educator with the longer history of Black teachers in Chicago. Elizabeth was, admittedly, in awe.

She was even more thrilled when Karen and Jill asked her to help write the memoir. The three of us agreed that Karen would start by freewriting material. Jill would provide prompts to help guide Karen's writing and structure the memoir. Elizabeth would write the historical context necessary for framing Karen's stories. Jill and Elizabeth would both read Karen's drafts and provide feedback. We proceeded in this way for several months, meeting periodically at Karen's CTU office and at her home to check in and talk through content and process. Elizabeth recorded the stories Karen shared during these meetings so that we could include them in the memoir.

This changed after October 2017, when Karen suffered a stroke. Karen was already a cancer survivor, and while we were terribly worried about her health and recovery, she was apologizing to us for being late with her drafts! Although Karen was no longer able to write after this health setback, she was as determined as ever to finish her memoir. So, we shifted. The memoir would have to be finished in a different way.

Over several years, we visited with Karen more than a dozen times to record interviews and conversations for this book. Karen's dear husband, John, was often present for our visits and welcomed us. We spent time with Karen at her presidential office, in the warmth of her South Side home, in downtown Chicago at the Shirley Ryan AbilityLab as she recovered from her stroke, and at Whitehall, the skilled nursing facility in Deerfield, Illinois, where she stayed after another round of surgery in 2018 when her cancer returned. We crafted a book proposal and eventually signed a book contract with Haymarket Books, codifying Karen's request that Elizabeth coauthor the memoir.

Elizabeth recorded her last in-person interview with Karen in February 2020, just before the pandemic shut everything down. While we couldn't meet in person anymore, Elizabeth started organizing the many hours of transcripts into rough book chapters. On February 7, 2021, after an extended battle with cancer, Karen passed away. This was a deeply sad time for the many people who loved Karen and the movement she led. People across the city and country grieved and mourned. The book stalled after Karen's passing. We were sad that Karen wouldn't get to see her memoir through to the end. But talking and meeting with John renewed our resolve to finish it. The work would have to pivot again.

Over time, we created processes to leverage the wealth of our recorded conversations. Using the interviews as the foundation, the Karen Lewis Memoir Team grew to include Marya Spont-Lemus (our incredibly talented transcriptionist, who easily tracked multiple voices and captured slang and code switches seamlessly), Sekordri Ojo (Elizabeth's indefatigable, resourceful graduate assistant and a former high school student of Karen's), and Summer McDonald (our nimble editor, who helped to chisel away at a very long early manuscript draft like a block of beautiful marble). In later drafts, John, Robert Bloch, Stacy Davis Gates, and Jesse Sharkey provided help in explaining timelines and clarifying detailed points. And Julie Fain, Katy O'Donnell, and the Haymarket Books team embraced this project with care throughout. Thank you to Joy Hoppenot for copy editing.

This book is a memoir: Karen Lewis's first-person memories and (re)tellings of her life. As Karen's coauthor, Elizabeth wrote material to provide continuity and necessary context, but she made a commitment to use Karen's very own words in the book, including Karen's original writing and the transcripts from our conversations. These are Karen's recollections of her experiences over time. The opinions expressed within this book are Karen's personal views, not official positions of the CTU or anyone else. Where dialogue appears, it was reconstructed to the best of Karen's recollection, re-creating the essence of conversations, rather than verbatim quotes. Others who were present may recall things differently. But this is Karen's story.

Luckily, most of the conversations that we recorded and transcribed before Karen passed away focused on her childhood and personal life—parts of her life that Elizabeth could not have accessed through other avenues. Still, holes in the narrative remained. Many of these gaps were from Karen's more public-facing years as CTU president. To write out these parts of her life more fully, Elizabeth drew on Karen's first-person writing from her monthly President's Message in the CTU's *Chicago Union Teacher* newsletter. Jill and Elizabeth recorded additional conversations with John to gain clarity and greater context for important moments in her adult life. Elizabeth included contextual elements from these interviews in the memoir as well. Sekordri and Elizabeth also scoured the Internet for videos of Karen's speeches, commentary, and interviews.

In this memoir, Karen's words from presidential columns, speeches, and other unpublished first-person writing and comments are integrated into the text without attribution. However, her comments from published interviews are cited. As the book developed, Elizabeth was increasingly grateful that she'd spent so much time listening to Karen speaking, both in person and on tape. This allowed her to learn Karen's voice and to appreciate the strong sense of orality in Karen's written work. In later rounds of revision, Jill and Elizabeth harnessed that knowledge to help edit her spoken words into a cohesive narrative (rather than a long and lively transcript). During the time we worked together on this project, Karen's health declined, but she was as profound and engaging as ever. Our conversations were punctuated by her laughter, spicy (and sometimes off-the-record) asides, side-eyes, giggles, and wonderful anecdotes about her love of tennis, opera, and travel. She was quite clear with us about who should—and should not—play her in any movies based on this book. Karen pulled no punches. She sharply critiqued policies and policymakers she disagreed with, she dreamed and planned for a better world, and she demonstrated vulnerability in sharing personal stories about her childhood, spirituality, and family.

So many people felt connected to Karen—this was one of her many superpowers. When she held court in a room, it was electric. On and off the record, Karen invited us to get to know KG (what her closest friends called her) and her more private side. As she told us on one of our visits, "You are getting a chance to be around *just me* . . . Not 'Karen Lewis.'" And of course, because it was Karen's way, she also became a friend and mentor to us. Karen was brilliant and poignant and absolutely hilarious. She told us how much fun she had working on this book. As she navigated health challenges, this book project gave her something to look forward to. It brought her joy. We're so grateful to have had the opportunity to laugh, cry, reflect, and learn with this once-in-a-lifetime leader. We hope that people who knew Karen will connect with her again as they hear her voice and stories in these pages. And that people who never had that chance will get to learn from this master teacher and be inspired by Karen's political courage, insights, and commitment to fighting for and building a better world. May Karen's memory be a blessing for us all.

Introduction

The world changed for me on Sunday, October 5, 2014. That morning, I attended a lovely community breakfast at a couple's home on the North Side of Chicago. The couple's children had attended Lane Tech High School, one of the largest and oldest public high schools in Chicago. I had taught chemistry at Lane for many years. The breakfast was a stop on my listening tour of the city's seventy-seven neighborhoods as I prepared to run for mayor.

Rahm Emanuel, the incumbent mayor, may have had President Barack Obama's encouragement and backing, but the polls were predicting a close race between us. That summer, the *Chicago Sun-Times* had me running about nine points ahead of Rahm, and I stayed ahead in most of the polls as Rahm's unpopularity continued to grow. I hadn't officially entered the race, but the American Federation of Teachers (AFT) had promised to pledge $1 million to my campaign if I decided to run.[1]

On that October morning, I listened intently to a group of middle-income couples discuss the vision they had for Chicago. These predominantly white North Siders were horrified about the governance of our city and were seeking other approaches to the issues—education was just one topic we discussed. From what I experienced, Rahm had a control-and-command style of governance that was undemocratic. Elites beholden to the mayor wielded power in the city. You could hear their voices in what came out of city hall, not the voices of the people of the city of Chicago. And Rahm's policies reflected this. He supported privatizing public education and other public services and promoted policies that disrupted school communities and entire neighborhoods. He closed public mental health clinics and public schools.[2] Combatting poverty and violence, increasing access to health care—these things were important to my supporters and our communities.

I left the breakfast meeting energized but exhausted. I went home, took a nap, and readied myself for the next stop: the same type of meeting, this one in the predominantly Black South Side neighborhood of South Shore, about forty minutes away from my first engagement that day.

I arrived at the home of Deborah Harrington with my dear friend and campaign manager, Jay Travis, a brilliant Black woman and organizer whom I trusted and adored. The home was a spacious vintage South Side apartment that featured gorgeous hardwood floors, charming architectural details, and tastefully arranged furniture. Harrington is a well-known philanthropist and activist in Chicago and was the first Black woman to lead the Woods Fund, a foundation that centers racial and economic justice in its grantmaking. Soon after we arrived, Jay insisted I accompany her to our host's bathroom. "Let's have a little water," she said, looking concerned. As I tried to drink, the water dribbled down my jaw. "We're going to the hospital. Right now." Jay thought I was having a stroke.

Mercy Hospital, a small teaching hospital just south of downtown, was about a fifteen-minute drive from Deborah's apartment and closer to my own South Side home in Bronzeville. The Mercy Hospital emergency room wasn't particularly crowded, and I was given an immediate EKG and CT scan. Imagine my shock when an ER nurse told me, "You have a brain tumor." I heard these words in the distorted slow-motion voice featured in movies.

§

Just a few years earlier, I had been catapulted onto the national political stage. I was elected president of the Chicago Teachers Union (CTU) in 2010, the third-largest teachers' union local in the country and the largest in Illinois. Two years later, I led the first teachers' strike in a quarter century in the adopted hometown of the sitting president. As Obama entered the final leg of his reelection campaign in 2012, we challenged the neoliberal policies of Rahm Emanuel, his former chief of staff, who had been elected mayor of Chicago in 2011. There was tremendous pressure from establishment forces in the Democratic Party—locally and nationally—not to strike. But we didn't back down.

We fought for the schools and communities our teachers, students, and families deserved. We boldly called out poverty and racism as the root causes of many of the challenges in our schools and demanded smaller class sizes, fully staffed schools with social workers and nurses, air conditioning, and fair compensation for our members. At mass marches during the strike, our members and community called out Rahm—and President Obama—directly with their signs and chants: "Hey, Rahm! Teachers don't like bullies!"; "Hey, Rahm, we're no fools! We won't let you ruin our schools!"; "President Obama, we're under attack! Was this your plan when you sent Rahm back?"; and, of course, "Hey, hey! Ho, ho! Rahm Emanuel's got to go!" While the strike has been called one of the most significant of the twenty-first century and was absolutely one of the most intense periods in my life, it was by no means my toughest battle. On Sunday, October 5, 2014, I was diagnosed with an aggressive, stage-four brain tumor. That Wednesday, I had an operation to cut it out. My plan to run for mayor was derailed.

In a way, I *wasn't* afraid. I named the tumor Porky because it looked like a pork chop. It had to go because, after all, I'm a Jew and pork isn't kosher. Mercy Hospital didn't have a neurosurgery department, so I had to transfer to Northwestern Hospital.

When I woke up from surgery, everyone with whom I am closest was at my bedside looking very grim. I felt fine. I had gotten the best rest and wasn't exhausted. My husband, John, sat on the bed, held my hand, and smiled at me, his big, beautiful brown eyes letting me know that everything was going to be fine. It wasn't until I saw my neurosurgeon the following day that I found out I had a glioblastoma—a very aggressive form of brain cancer. My heart sank. I had lost one of my closest friends to that horrible disease. When she was diagnosed, I made immediate plans to see her in California as I knew she had, at best, two years to live. I thought I'd been handed the same death sentence as my friend. I was sixty-one when I got my diagnosis. At that moment, I thought I'd never see another birthday.

But the neurosurgeon convinced me I had some things in my favor, including my general good health and Porky's location. Almost three years after surgery, my neuro-oncologist took me out of the short-term survival category and put me on the long-term list instead. She told me her longest surviving glioblastoma patient is ten years out from diagnosis. I plan to shatter that number! I want to dance at my great-granddaughter's wedding.

Through the whole ordeal, there was only one moment when I *really* thought I was gonna die, and that's when I got a text from

Rahm Emanuel from a number I didn't recognize. First, it just freaked me out because I was still in the hospital. Then I said to myself, "Oh my God, his brother Zeke [who is a doctor] told him I was dying, and now he's happy as hell because he knows I can't continue in the mayoral race." Because I was whipping his ass in the polls. The cancer may have stopped me from running for mayor, but it didn't stop *me*!

§

As I continued to serve as CTU president, people always asked me to do blurbs for their books, and I thought, "I want my own damn book!" I've always liked writing. When I was a kid, I used to write letters all the time. My parents gave me this old typewriter. It was one of those big ones with the keys that really *clop-clop-clop*. My love of writing showed up in school too. I was always one of the kids who wanted the teachers to like my work. And I'm still like that.

In writing this book, I wanted to do it well. I had a lot of things to say about the so-called education reformers and I wanted to write about policy. I also wanted to dig into race and class. But it had to be fun, so I try to keep it personal and funny while saying things that I think people still need to hear. I see myself as a storyteller, and I wanted to tell stories because that's how life happens. I want people to hear my voice. I've enjoyed the process of writing and creating this book. My hope is that this book shows my evolution—from a socially active kid into a labor leader who led the first successful large strike in America in many, many years.

My life has been truly remarkable, and it has been shaped by my curiosity as well as an innate drive to build fairness. Some have called me a seeker, and my explorations started early. I traveled to Paris as a preteen and organized Black Power walkouts in high school. In spite of my mother's initial objections, I left high school a year early and attended Mount Holyoke College in the early 1970s, an experience that transformed me. I transferred to Dartmouth College in 1972 and was the only Black woman in the class of 1974. I had a short but unsuccessful stint in medical school, lived in Barbados for a year, married young, and became a widow while still in my thirties.

But I found my passion in the classroom. I taught for more than twenty years before becoming a union leader in Chicago, the most political city in the nation. After knowing him for a decade, I married my dear husband, life partner, and fellow high school teacher, John Lewis, in 2001. And I converted to Judaism and found a new grounding in my spirituality later in life.

I served as CTU president for eight years, from 2010 to 2018. After my retirement, I watched the wave of #RedforEd strikes—in places like Arizona, Colorado, Los Angeles, Oklahoma, Virginia, and West Virginia—and social justice union organizing around the nation with a sense of pride. What we built in Chicago impacted teachers across the country and shifted the narrative about teachers and public education. We'd lived through the ravages of the corporate takeover of public education: high stakes and overtesting, divestment from public schools, the demonization of teachers, and the expansion of charter schools that undermined existing public schools.

In *I Didn't Come Here to Lie*, I document the personal and professional journeys that made me into a labor leader, an advocate for public education and for children, and a symbol of the progressive Left. I reflect on how my family, education, spirituality, and activism helped me navigate my life and leadership. I write candidly about my political commitments to teachers, children, and community and the important role that self-education, faith, friendship, and family have played over the course of my life. I recall these events to make space for other people to come through behind me. I can't hold on to all of this and not pass it along to somebody else! That would be selfish. The only way I know how to tell this story is to be honest and open and just tell the truth.

Chapter 1

There's Nothing Stopping You

There are tons of things I cannot remember, but other memories are still vividly chasing me through my adulthood. My most important childhood memories include hanging out with my dad. My father, a protofeminist, shielded me from misogyny and constantly told me, "You can do anything you want to. There's nothing stopping you."

When I said, "Well, can I play baseball?" he said, "Sure!" When I was six, he taught me how to bat, and he taught me how to bat left-handed. "You're right-handed. But if you bat left-handed—remember this—in the major leagues, right field is always shorter. So it will give you an advantage." He never told me major league baseball was inaccessible to girls. When I was eight, he took me to an all-star football game at Soldier Field. I said, "Daddy, there are no girls playing football." "Don't worry about that. When you get grown, there will be girls playing football."

I was born on July 20, 1953, in the Chicago Lying-In Hospital at the University of Chicago, so I've been a Hyde Parker from birth. I came in three weeks early because I guess I got tired of sitting around in there and doing nothing. When babies are ready to make their appearance, they do. And you can't make them come any faster than they want to. I was ready to go. I was like, "Let me *ouuut*!" According to my father, it was the hottest day of the year. My mother claims she doesn't remember how hot it was, so I'll go with his version.

My parents are not from Chicago. My mother, Martha Jennings (née Gaikins), is from Saint Louis, the youngest of five daughters. My maternal grandfather, Dr. George Alvin Gaikins, was born in Arkansas around 1892. I never met him because he died when I was just three weeks old. I only knew him by what my mother and my aunts said about him. Some of their stories are not so true, while some of them are *overly* true. There was a whole lot of mythmaking around him because he was a surgeon. And how many Black surgeons were there in those days? He graduated from Philander Smith College in 1916 and Howard University medical school in 1921. He was one of the first Black professors at Washington University School of Medicine in Saint Louis and was a surgeon at Homer G. Phillips Hospital, the only public hospital for Black people in Saint Louis at the time. He trained many Black surgeons who went through Homer G. Phillips Hospital, up until he died of a heart attack in 1953.

The stories I heard never made me think he was anything but an autocratic, cheap, cranky man. I heard that he was penurious and that he kept his gum and his cigars in a little locked case. He split a stick of gum five ways to teach his daughters the importance of either sharing or thrift. I'm not sure which, but in any event, five ways? That's crazy to me!

And to my young eyes, in photos my grandfather looked exactly like Adolf Hitler. *Exactly* like him. Down to the mustache. When I was a little girl and saw pictures of him, he scared me. I would say to my mother, "This was your father? Why does he look like Adolph Hitler?" And she would explain that it was the style back then, to have those little mustaches. I said, "Ohhhh, no. If he were my husband, he'd have to change that." I don't know why my grandma let him do that. I mean, they lived through World War II together, you know?

My maternal grandmother, also named Martha, was from Clifton Forge, Virginia. Because she lived until 1989, when I was in my mid-thirties, I knew her very well. She came and lived with us when my sister, Keli, was born. Each time one of her daughters—my aunts—had a baby, my grandmother would go to their house and stay with them for a while. Keli is ten years younger than me, so I remember that time well. I remember my grandmother bathing Keli in the sink, and I would just watch her. She was just super straight, a rule follower.

I also observed that my grandmother was a race woman, in interesting and contradictory ways. For one thing, she just *did not* trust white people—any of them. She did not like the fact that two of my best friends growing up were white girls. She never trusted them. But then, in my freshman year of high school, I wore an Afro, and my grandmother was absolutely outraged by my choice. I was confused. She didn't want me to have an Afro—cute and a symbol of Black pride—yet she also didn't want me to have white friends. Not at all.

From stories I've heard, I think my grandmother's father was probably white. She would never talk about it. I think it was something she was ashamed of. *Very* ashamed. Talking about it would mean she'd have to admit to illegitimacy. And that was painful for her.

I remember once, we were at my cousin Tootsie's house in Washington, DC. Tootsie had a pool, and my grandmother would sit on the side of the pool and put her legs in. I said, "Grandma, come on in and swim!" She never would. And she said, "I don't know how to swim." When I said, "We'll teach you!" she said no. She was a little afraid of the water, but she enjoyed it, and she enjoyed all the grandkids and great-grandkids splashing around. I asked her, "Well, why don't you know how to swim, Grandma?"

"Because when I grew up, colored couldn't swim at the pool. They could only swim in the creek." Her life must have been so damn tough. And I just look back at it, thinking about her sitting on the side of that pool—I will never forget that—wistfully looking into that water, wishing. You could tell she wished she had learned to swim.

My father, Geoffrey Jennings, may he rest in peace, was from Tulsa, Oklahoma. My father was born in 1926, the middle child of three boys. My paternal grandparents moved from Tulsa to Chicago during World War II to find better work. They actually moved to Detroit first and then settled in Chicago, because Chicago seemed better to them and more of a mecca for Black people. They weren't necessarily part of the Great Migration of Black people to Chicago in the most direct way, but they made their way here. I have always been fascinated by how Black people can pick up, start their lives over, and keep it going. We are a resilient people.

My paternal grandfather, William "Willie Ed" Jennings, was from Stringtown, Oklahoma. We called him Popeye, and he was probably born around 1906. He was the caretaker-slash-janitor at Saint James Methodist Church on Forty-Sixth and Ellis in Chicago. He was the cutest man ever and had a wild mane of hair. I don't know how true this is, but supposedly his mother was a Choctaw Indian named Lillian Houston. His father was a riverboat gambler and con man named Joe Jennings. His mother died when Willie Ed was two—I think she died in childbirth—so the only memory he had of her and of his sisters was of them combing their hair.

When I was a little kid, I would spend a lot of time with my grandfather. He saw specialness in me at early o'clock. I was the light of his eye. He would give me beer. Hell, he taught me how to drive when I was eight. He said I might need that skill. Years later, when my grandfather met my first husband, Arnold Leo Glenn, he told him, "Sonny, if anything happens to her, I'm coming after you, because that is my firstborn!" My first husband was six foot three and 230 pounds, but he would always tell me, "You know, I'm not scared of your dad. I'm not scared of your uncles. But I'm *terrified* of Popeye."

Until my sister, Keli, came along in 1963, I was an only child. But I had family *everywhere* and grew up around my older cousins and adult relatives. I think that's why I was so mature. My cousins didn't think of me as a little kid, because I was always around grown people. And I was *always* with my paternal grandmother, Laurene Jennings (née Baker), who we called Muddy. She would take me everywhere because she was showing me off. "There's my cute little granddaughter." Muddy would take me to all her friends' houses and she would take me to church.

Muddy's church, Bray Temple CME, was nothing like the Lutheran church where my parents took me. The Lutheran church reminded me of Catholic churches, but without any showbiz. Very dry. Muddy's church was more hand-clapping and shouting. "That's the truth!" Brother George, in the back, head of the *urshcrrr* board, shouting, "A-men!" I loved going to church with my grandmother for entertainment purposes. It was free entertainment. That's the thing I looked forward to. Otherwise, it was kind of boring to hang out with old people.

My parents met while they were in college. They were in a play together at Lincoln University, a historically Black university in Jefferson City, Missouri, that had been founded by a white abolitionist and Black soldiers born into slavery. My mother was attending Stowe Teachers College, a Black teachers' college in Saint Louis, when my parents first met. But she attended summer school at Lincoln where Daddy went to school. My mother and my father played brother and sister in this play. I think it was kind of romantic that my parents met in a play, even though they were playing brother and sister—they clearly developed some sort of closeness in that.

When my mother married my father, they came to Chicago because his parents had moved there; they had a big-ass house in Englewood. When my parents moved to Englewood in the early 1950s, the neighborhood was in flux; white people were starting to flee to the suburbs or other parts of the city as Black people from Chicago's South Side Black Belt—also known as Bronzeville, the initial destination in Chicago for many Southern Black migrants—were beginning to move in. In 1950, only 11 percent of the neighborhood's residents were Black, but by 1960, the neighborhood was 69 percent Black.[1] My mother didn't want to live in Englewood, but my father convinced her. "We can live here and save up for our own place." She understood that because my mother always understood money. She still does.

I lived in a very political house. My parents were socially conservative in some ways, but they also had radical politics. They belonged to the Congress of Racial Equality, they wrote checks to the National Association for the Advancement of Colored People (NAACP), and they were members of the Independent

Voters of Illinois. They were all about civil rights and they were all about equality. At the dinner table, we discussed the news every single day. I was always encouraged to push the limits on my intellect and my politics—even as a little kid. I mean, even if you were a kid, you better be in it, or you wouldn't have anything to say! Right above the dining room table, we had a map of the world and a map of the United States. My father would use the map to talk about World War II, what had happened in history, and what was happening currently all over the world. I remember him being fascinated by the Dardanelles, and I remember him talking about the Finns. As he told it, the Finns had held off the Russians during World War II until they just ran out of people. He said they were on skis, shooting folks. His stories were amazing, and they made all kinds of things come alive for me.

My father was a bit ahead of his time, and he intended for his care and attention to provide an advantage for me. One of the consequences was that as a young person, I didn't always understand sexism or gender bias—I was never told I couldn't do anything because I was a girl. Because being female never seemed like a barrier to me, I was confused by the women's movement some years later. I thought it was a middle-class white women's movement. Some of my own understandings of feminism only began to form later for me, in high school and college. And certainly, as a teacher and union leader, I saw how we were treated unfairly as teachers because more than 80 percent of us are women. As a feminized profession, we were both demonized and paternalized by those in power.

Given his generous and encouraging nature, it's not surprising that everybody loved my father. He was a storyteller and wired to connect with people. I think I get my curiosity, sociability, and confidence from him. He really wanted me to be Miss

America, which I thought was hilarious. My father pushed me to do better and be stronger, but not in order to please him. Instead, he emphasized the space I could take up. "You have an opportunity for things I didn't have because of racism," he would say, "so I want to make sure you have every opportunity."

On the other hand, my mother was controlling and more oriented toward appearances and managing how things looked. This was always challenging for me, because I don't give a shit what I look like to other people. But I still have so much in common with my mother. I look *exactly* like her. We're both strong-willed. We're both Cancers, which means we're also homebodies. And when I was very little, I was probably closer to her than I was to my father. I remember the two of us hanging out all the time back then. We would go down Fifty-Third Street together, we would shop, and we'd always stop at a bakery and get a sugar cookie or something before going home. I started hanging out more with my father when I got older because he was fun, just a ridiculous amount of fun.

Every Friday, I would put on a show for my parents, inspired by something I had seen in the movies. My father and I went to the movies all the time. We saw *Perri*, a Disney movie about a squirrel, and *The Bravados* with Gregory Peck, who was my first celebrity crush.

I didn't exactly feel free when I was a kid; I felt contained. But I was outgoing and an extrovert, and my parents loved and encouraged this. They never told me to sit down and shut up. They would never do that.

Chapter 2

My Black Chicago Childhood

Class for Black folks is complicated. When I was a little kid, I thought we were somewhere in the middle. My parents always said we were poor, but they didn't bother to explain the nuances of different statuses like working class, middle class, or elite. I knew we weren't rich, but it didn't seem like we were poor either. Some of my classmates teased me and called me "rich girl" because I didn't have any siblings until I was ten, and I had lots of toys, especially dolls.

When I was growing up, my family was one of the only Black families I knew where both parents were college educated. Even my closest friends might have had one college-educated parent, but not two. Both of my parents had bachelor's degrees—Daddy's degree was in industrial arts and Mommy's was in elementary education. On the one hand, they had achieved a level of education that some of the Black folks that I thought were rich did not have. But we were still in a different position financially.

Both my parents ended up as teachers, but they had not always worked as teachers. The 1950s was a harbinger of a new era; young, college-educated Negroes—which is what we were called back then—had hopeful expectations for the future. But my father could not get a job teaching high school then. He was qualified to teach woodshop, drafting, and architectural drawing, but there were only three Black high schools at the time, so he used his degree and skills and went into woodworking and light manufacturing. When I was a young child, my father worked in a shutter-making shop and my mother was a credit and collections specialist at Spiegel, the mail-order giant.

I didn't understand why my parents were always saying we were poor. Little kids would say to me, "You're rich!" I would come home and tell my parents, and they would start laughing their heads off. I knew we weren't on welfare, but I do remember going to the unemployment compensation office with my father when he was laid off from one of his jobs before he finally found a teaching job. But then we went right next door to my piano lessons. I had piano lessons, dance lessons, and art lessons. Even though I wasn't any good at art, I had the lessons.

My parents' experience speaks to the relationship between social class, economic class, and other status markers for Black folks. My parents had bachelor's degrees, but they were not rich or in any of the elite Black social clubs where Chicago's professional, business, civic, and socialite set gathered and gala-ed together. They weren't in the Druids. They weren't in the Royal Coterie of Snakes. They weren't in the Links. They weren't even really that involved with their sororities and fraternities. My mother was an AKA (Alpha Kappa Alpha) and my dad was a Kappa (Kappa Alpha Psi). But they weren't very involved in their chapters in Chicago when I was a kid.

Social class could be marked by what you prioritized, what religion you practiced, all types of things. When I asked my mother why I needed to have piano lessons when Daddy wasn't working, she said certain things were in the budget and other things weren't. New clothes for my parents weren't in the budget, but they would find a way for me to take piano lessons. It wasn't until I got older that I began to understand their choices, the sacrifices they made, and some of their life-altering decisions. They were not rich, but by virtue of the things and experiences they provided for me, they were trying to create different ways for me to move through the world. I thought we were middle class. And that's what my parents were striving for.

Growing up in Hyde Park, the neighborhood surrounding the University of Chicago, was a different experience than growing up in other South Side neighborhoods, at least in the 1950s and 1960s. It seemed like a more bohemian, laid-back community, and it shaped how I experienced race, class, and social status. When I was a child, Hyde Park seemed very integrated. What I did not realize at the time was that Hyde Park was segregated by blocks. White people lived in certain parts of Hyde Park. Asians lived on other blocks in Hyde Park. And we all went to different elementary schools. I went to the "worst" elementary school in Hyde Park, while my high school friends had gone to better-ranked schools. My elementary school, William C. Reavis, was the school that most of the Black children in Hyde Park attended. Even though it was considered a bad school, we had terrific programs, terrific teachers, and a fairly progressive educational outlook. While we were tracked, the tracking seemed fluid. You could go in and out of different classes. We didn't realize it, but we were living through a time of transition in Hyde Park.

By then, federally sponsored urban renewal plans were underway in the neighborhood, opposed by some people in Hyde Park, but strongly supported and shaped by the University of

Chicago. Beginning in the 1950s, these urban renewal projects were knocking down "blighted" buildings to build new housing for higher-income people, and many people felt forced to leave. Other Black families with the means to do so were moving to buy houses in recently desegregated neighborhoods just south of Hyde Park.[1] I had friends whose parents were doctors and lawyers who were much wealthier than us, and they were moving to South Shore into huge single-family houses in a very beautiful tree-lined community called The Highlands. Even if you don't know a thing about Chicago, the name certainly sounds tony.

As people moved, I would ask my friends, "Why are *we* still stuck here in Hyde Park? Why can't *we* move to South Shore?" South Shore seemed like the better place. But my family lived in a two-flat in Hyde Park that my parents owned, and we always had tenants, which meant that my parents had income coming in from the downstairs apartment. In a single-family house, you have no extra income; you're just paying for everything. I didn't understand this as a child, but my parents were able to make things work where we were because of the income from the tenants.

§

My first school was Cosmopolitan Nursery School on Fifty-Third and Wabash. They are in a newer building now, but the church that housed the school is still there. My teacher was a beautiful young woman named Miss Betty. I loved her and she seemed to love me. The principal, Miss Cook, was a rigid disciplinarian with whom I meshed about as well as oil with water. When you got in trouble, you had to sit at Miss Cook's table instead of sitting with your classmates and Miss Betty at lunch. After spending so many lunches in trouble at Miss Cook's table, I decided to make the best of it. I used my charm, my wit, and my smile to engage her. I sat up straight, minded my table manners, and asked her questions about herself. I remember finding out that she lived in Lake Meadows, a rather fancy set of high-rise apartments which housed quite a few of the Black elite—doctors, lawyers, and real estate and insurance moguls. These new apartments were built as part of an urban renewal project where they demolished the slums of the old Black Belt. Needless to say, Lake Meadows was out of reach for my parents.

My first day of kindergarten at William C. Reavis Elementary, I came home crying bitterly. My great-aunt Maurene (my grandma Muddy's twin sister) lived across the street from Reavis in a big old house, which is now a park, Jessie "Ma" Houston Park. This part of the neighborhood is where Hyde Park meets Bronzeville—the community where lots of Black folks initially settled when they migrated to Chicago from the South. In those days, the park had these huge mansions sitting on it that people had bought up and subdivided into smaller apartments. My aunt was babysitting me after school because kindergarten was only half a day. When my mother picked me up and saw me crying, she asked me what happened. "They didn't teach me to read!" That's what I had been looking forward to. I mean, I was *wrecked*. "What are we playing in the sand for? Why are we playing in this little house thing? Why are we taking a nap? I could do *all* this at home." I thought reading was the whole purpose of school. I'd heard that when you go to school, you learn to read. I was tired of being dependent on my parents reading me bedtime stories. If I learned to read, I wouldn't need my parents to read to me at night. I could read to myself, which would have been another step toward independence. I wanted to have a voice. I wanted to be *seen*. I wanted to be *respected.*

I really didn't like kindergarten, but even if they weren't going to teach me how to read, I truly needed the socialization required by learning with and playing with other children. As an only child at that time, I liked things my way. My kindergarten report card is funny as hell. It said I was bossy. I resented it! I told my mother, "I have good ideas! I don't make kids follow along with what I want to do, but if I have good ideas, well, why am I supposed to be quiet about it?" My mother replied gently, "You know, Karen, you *do* have a tendency to tell the other children what to do." "Because I have good ideas!" I insisted. I thought schools were supposed to recognize leadership. I didn't tell the kids they were stupid or anything. Why didn't the lady say I exhibited leadership skills? No, she said I was bossy. That's kinda wrong, you know.

That was my start as a leader, bossing other children around in kindergarten. I didn't mean any harm. I just thought there were other ways to accomplish goals. Mostly, though, I thought of myself as an organizer. I was so happy when kindergarten was over. I was ecstatic. How is it that a five-year-old knows when her time is being wasted? I could never understand why people treat kindergartners as if they are stupid. They are not!

For the record, I hated being a little kid. I felt pushed and pulled, tossed and turned, but mostly completely out of control. I had no rights—only tons of rules and regulations I had to follow, which often felt arbitrary and confusing. I felt as if I were being remolded in someone else's image. I didn't know at the time that I was learning how to resist a life of compliance. Mostly, life seemed incredibly unfair to me. "Wait 'til you're older" was a constant refrain in my house. I could never get a definitive answer as to what age that might be. I felt an enormous sense of oppression at not being allowed to express my deepest held convictions, or when the arbitrariness of the latest rule left me in tears trying to explain my side. When I got asked, "Why did you do that?" I often tried to come up with an answer that would satisfy my parents.

I finally felt liberated when I could honestly say, "Because I wanted to." By then, I had figured out that I could deal with whatever punishment they would mete out. I calculated the odds of what I could tolerate. I couldn't handle much physical pain (fortunately, my parents weren't from the "beat you down" school), but two weeks without television? No problem. I always had my books, in which I could fantasize being in a family that did wonderful, exotic things—going on safaris, elk hunting in Canada, living in the Caribbean. I wanted to be heard and to be understood. That was so important to me.

My first-grade teacher really taught me how to read. And I adored her for it. Her name was Audrey Marchbanks, and she was gorgeous, beautiful, and kind. I actually thought she was a movie star and she had just come to the school to do some community service work. She had all these skills—she could sing, she could draw—I mean, she could do everything. She also played the piano beautifully. In those days, in order to teach primary grades, you had to be able to play the piano. We had music every morning after "My Country, 'Tis of Thee" and the Pledge of Allegiance. Then we'd have some reading and math, but we'd always have music. At least twice a week we had art in the afternoon. Mrs. Marchbanks was also a brilliant artist. She was the kind of person who just encouraged you. I could never draw, but she would still tell me how wonderful my stuff was. She didn't care what it looked like. But the most important thing she did was teach me how to read, which made me a completely different human being.

In the middle of second grade, I got in a fight with this boy named Earl, and I got kicked out of Reavis because I didn't live in the attendance boundary. I got sent to Charles Kozminski Elementary, about four blocks south of Reavis. At the time, there were a few white kids left at Kozminski, but most of them had left as more Black kids came to the school. By the time I was in eighth grade, Kozminski was more than 95 percent Black.[2] If you looked at the older class pictures from Kozminski, you could see how integrated it used to be.

This was around the time in the early 1960s that Black folks in Chicago were fighting against segregation in the public schools. Schools serving Black children were overcrowded and under-resourced, and Chicago Public Schools (CPS) superintendent Benjamin Willis—who served in the role from 1953 to 1966—made it nearly impossible for Black students to attend underenrolled, predominantly white schools with open seats. Instead, the board of education gerrymandered attendance areas, created policies that made it hard to transfer, and installed portable trailers at Black schools to deal with overcrowding and maintain segregation by keeping Black kids in their all-Black schools. Black parents and community groups organized against these trailers—called "Willis Wagons" after the segregationist superintendent.[3] As a kid I wasn't aware of all of this, but I remember attending classes in portable classrooms. And I also remember when I first experienced racism in the classroom.

My third-grade teacher at Kozminski was white and extremely prejudiced. This was my first experience with racism, and I knew something was wrong. The student population at Kozminski might have been 95 percent Black, but the teaching staff was not. I noticed that my white third-grade teacher treated the little white girls very differently than how she treated everybody else. They were allowed to do things she didn't allow anybody else to do. And of course, I had attributed it to something else—to them having long hair.

She had a real dislike of kids not writing big on the board. When she would send us to the board to do our math problems, if you didn't write really big, she would make you sit down. All little kids, unless they're overwhelmingly shy, like going to the board. The little white girls would always draw small on the board, but she never made them sit down or punished them for it. The scientist in me took over, and I decided, "I'm going to do a test." I always wrote big on the board, but one day, I decided to write small. I made sure I mimicked the size of the white girls' numerals. No smaller than they wrote, but no larger. The teacher made me sit down. And I said, "But you didn't make Anna or Jane sit down."

I was outraged, and I told my mother about it. I would always tell my mother that the teacher was unfair. I didn't know it was racism back then, but I always thought she was very unfair. My mother said that she would see about it, but when she attended the open house, the teacher complained to my mother: "I've never seen a child that's so concerned about fairness. She's always talking about what's fair and what's not fair." My mother said, "Isn't that a wonderful quality in one so young?" This was the first time my mother had *ever* stood up for me. She stood up for me because she knew what it was.

I thought that was very interesting, as I look back. You know, about how I handled it, how my mother handled it. Because my mother was one of those who would say, "Whatever the teacher says, you're in the wrong." "Just do what you're told" was her attitude about most things. But when she heard that story, she knew I was reacting to something wrong, for real. And my mother realized it was racism. But she didn't tell *me* it was. Because my parents didn't want me hurt by telling me that at an early age. My parents protected me from a lot of that stuff.

At that moment, my parents affirmed my feelings without giving up all the info. What a trick! They wanted their kids to stay *whole*, but they didn't want to deny what I was experiencing. It's all a lab. Trying things out as parents, trying things out as kids. Like the science I pulled on that teacher. "Let me test! Let me test it! Make sure that I'm not just imagining this." As a little kid, you never know what's real because you live so much of your life in your imagination.

I'm a fighter by nature. I will *fight* insincerity. I will *fight* bullshit. I will *fight* unfairness. That's why I had so much trouble with my parents, because a lot of the stuff they did seemed very arbitrary and unfair. And if something is unfair, you gotta fight that. I remember my mother not being happy with me about pushing back on her. I would say, "Well, if you didn't want me to think, why did you teach me how to think?" Well, she didn't say anything to that because she had nothing to say! "*You* taught me how to think." And she had! She *knew* she had. I said, "How do you expect me not to think when *you* taught me to think? You thought I wasn't going to use it against you?"

Chapter 3

The Consciousness-Raising Years

While I attended public schools in Chicago starting in kindergarten, the only CPS school that I actually graduated from was Kozminski Elementary School, named for Charles Kozminski, a nineteenth-century banker and Chicago school board member, located at Fifty-Fourth and Ingleside in Hyde Park. In 1967, I graduated from eighth grade.

That July, my French teacher, Madame Webster, accompanied a group of students to France for two weeks. I had been taking French since the fourth grade, and this was the culminating event of Madame Webster's experiment. It was an experience most of us will never forget.

Madame Webster decided that it was important for us to go to France, especially because Kozminski was always looked down upon as a "shitty" school in Hyde Park. And, frankly, it was. But Madame Webster designed this outstanding French language program and took a big group of students—about thirty of us—to tour the Loire valley. We were a group of mostly Black kids going to France—there were about six white kids in the bunch. And as young teenagers who had just graduated, we were so excited.

I'd been looking forward to being out from under the watchful eyes of my parents. Unfortunately for me, both of them chaperoned the trip. The good thing was that neither of my parents spoke French, so they had to rely on me for help. All they knew how to say was, "How much does this cost?" and "good morning," "goodbye," and "thank you."

Madame Webster had *beautiful* salt-and-pepper hair, and she was so nurturing. She taught French for many years within CPS and was later known to lucky students at other elementary schools in Hyde Park. She gave us all French names. At first I was Jeanne, but I didn't like it. I wanted to be Marie-Hélène, something with a little more pizzazz. By the time I got to seventh grade, she let me change it. I still use the French that I learned then. She did not allow us to use books. Instead, we listened to records—*les disques*—and parroted the Parisian French.

I like to tell people, "I started French in the fourth grade, just listening to records." I *still* remember those dialogues. The key is that when you start that early, you develop better comprehension and speaking skills. It was all about listening and understanding. Hearing and speaking. It was called the audio-lingual method—ALM. I am often surprised by Francophones who are shocked to hear a Black American speak French without an American accent. And they are even more shocked to discover that I am a product of the Chicago Public Schools and that high-quality French classes were offered to me in elementary school so many years ago. That was when a teacher with a great idea and a supportive principal could pull off miracles.

This was my first big trip. Our family vacations and excursions were to Saint Louis or Washington, DC—that's where we had family. It wasn't my first time on a plane, though. I'd flown to DC when I was younger. I'd found it funny because my father was so afraid of flying that he got drunk. On the trip to France, we flew Air France from Chicago to Montreal, then we changed planes in Montreal. I thought that being at the airport in Montreal was one of the coolest things ever because most of the signs were in French! In Montreal, we had a chance to work on reading signs and get ready to use our French.

We arrived in Paris around eight or ten in the morning, and we were all completely wiped out. I don't know who arranged that trip—maybe it was Madame Webster herself, with help from contacts in France—but our itinerary was *so cool.* We spent the first couple of days in Paris, doing the typical touristy Paris stuff, like going to the Louvre. Then we got on a coach bus that took us *allll* the way around the Loire valley. We would drive to a château, get out, go look at the château, get back in, get a boxed lunch someplace—which was usually bread and some meat, maybe some cheese. I mean, we got so sick of châteaus—it was *all* about the châteaus. But I did have a favorite one. I really liked Chenonceau in the Loire valley.

While it didn't feel hostile, everywhere we went, people looked at us like, "Who are these little children?" The first couple of days we were there, when we were in Paris, they had hooked us up with some pretty upper-class, aristocratic French families. We just visited with them for the day to get a sense of what life in Paris was like—I didn't like them at all, because they seemed snobbish and not truly friendly. But they lived in these *beautiful* apartments, with the tallest ceilings I had ever seen. They were tall like the ceilings in the gym, but with beautiful art and tapestries on the wall. It felt like these apartments were museums! After seeing this, we didn't have to go to the Louvre. But, of course, we went to the Louvre too.

For my parents, one of the trip's highlights was the day we met Josephine Baker—the Black American expatriate, entertainer, and a renowned figure in France. My parents were all goofy about it—she meant something special to them; here's a Saint Louis girl who had made it *big*—but I didn't really know who she was until I recognized one of her songs. I still don't know how Madame Webster arranged that visit. Baker was living in this château—Château des Milandes—and she'd adopted kids from all over the world. They were all running around looking like little ragamuffins. While the adults spent time talking to Ms. Baker, we played with the children. Ms. Baker's sister, Margaret, also known as Meg, had moved there from Saint Louis. My mother, also from Saint Louis, spent some time talking to her. Meg's attitude was more like, "You know that's all a façade, right?" She gave us the behind-the-scenes look, and the lowdown on Ms. Baker's world, but in a way that was kind. She wasn't dismissive or cheeky; she was more like, "wink-wink, nod-nod." That was a fun day. My parents were in awe of Ms. Baker and the whole scene.

My parents were in awe of everything. I was especially tickled by that—it felt like the first time my parents were *proud* of me. Here I was, moving among all of these different kinds of people, speaking French, organizing things—doing things that they couldn't do. I had a certain independence there, and they recognized that. The best thing was that the day before we left France to go back home, I turned fourteen. And I just knew I was grown up. On my birthday, I spent an entire day alone in Paris doing grown-up things like shopping and having coffee. I bought a little dress that I thought was very chic and these cool purple patent-leather shoes with little silver buckles on them. I wore those things until I lost them. After I finished shopping,

I made my way back to the youth hostel on the Metro, alone and triumphant. The whole trip was incredibly fun and joyful, a transformative adventure for many of us. My friends and I were allowed to do grown-up things, but with some protections afforded to us as children.

I've reflected on how that experience, and others like it, shaped me. These kinds of exposures are really important. If you're given responsibility early in life, this can prepare you to lead later. I really didn't like being a kid—too many directives ("do this," "do that," "don't do this")—and I did not like feeling like I didn't have much control over my life. But in Paris, I experienced a little freedom and took on more responsibility. My relationship with my parents changed after the trip to France. I was always trying to figure out how to get *back* there and, relatedly, how I could get away from my parents. I got a glimpse of wider possibilities for myself there. And after that summer, it was *very* clear to me that there was a way out.

§

In 1967, the year that I graduated from elementary school, Dr. King was still alive and lots of stuff was going on—the Vietnam War, the antiwar movement, Civil Rights and Black Power movements, and liberation struggles all over the world. All of that energy was bubbling up in '67. And I was seeing, and resisting, the idea of white people having so much privilege. It was clear for me, even at an early age, that white people had privileges that Black people did not have. *We* got punished for things that white people didn't get punished for. I used to think when I was a kid how lucky I was that I grew up in Chicago and not in the South—until I heard Malcolm X say, "Long as you south of the

Canadian border, you're South."[1] That's deep. It's true, too. This is the world we lived in and the things I was thinking about when I started my freshman year at Kenwood High School.

Kenwood had only been open as a high school for one year when I started attending in the fall of 1967. The high school operated in the building that had previously housed Kenwood Elementary School. To make room for the new high school students, they moved the elementary school kids to other area elementary schools. Kenwood accepted its first incoming class of high school freshmen in 1966. It was planned and designed as an intentionally integrated school, to be attractive to white families in the Hyde Park and Kenwood neighborhoods who were fleeing Hyde Park High School; those families would not send their kids to other nearby high schools because those were already nearly all Black too. CPS built a new school building for Kenwood High School at the corner of Blackstone Avenue and Hyde Park Boulevard, but we didn't move into the new building until my junior year in September 1969. When I attended Kenwood, it was about 65 percent Black, 26 percent white, and 8 percent Asian American.[2]

Who I am as a human being—my values, principles, and political views—are rooted in my days as a student. I think I always gravitated to the kids who were a little more radical, which made sense given that my parents were fairly political. I hung out with a very integrated group of students at Kenwood, mostly Black girls, kind of bougie like myself, some even bougier, and some of the radical white lefty boys; I'm still in contact with some of them. My closest buddy of that time was a kid named Geoffrey Mirelowitz, and we're still good friends. The white kids were very much antiracist, but they didn't know how to participate because they didn't feel comfortable; they weren't about appropriating Black spaces, and they were very respectful, which was unusual. They manifested their activism via antiwar activism. We came together with antiwar organizing and activism against anti-Black racism, which was pretty unusual back then. We had coalitions. Black students at Kenwood had grievances similar to Black students at other schools. We wanted more Black teachers and administrators. We wanted to learn Black history in school. We wanted better resources and opportunities for Black students. And we were active at Kenwood and across the city.

The Black student movement was a citywide movement, and it seemed to me that it was more active and vibrant on the West Side than the South Side. I think this was because many of the West Side kids were coordinated by and connected to Fred Hampton, chairman of the Illinois chapter of the Black Panther Party. I idolized him and the Panthers because they were so passionate about justice and caring for Black communities, and they tried to do things the right way. When I was in high school, I went to several very large gatherings they organized on the West Side.

Like many Black folks I knew on the South Side, I didn't know anything about the West Side. I could get from my house to downtown on public transportation, but I hadn't gone on my own to neighborhoods on the West Side. When I wanted to go to a meeting there, my parents would drive. They were always the schleppers, especially my dad. They wanted to chaperone, and they would include other kids who were interested. My parents were supportive of my activism. They themselves were pretty engaged—with the Congress of Racial Equity and the NAACP. They wouldn't march, but they'd write checks, host meetings, and stay informed. That's the kind of activism they engaged in because they were cautious. They were always like, "Don't get arrested. I don't care what you do, just don't get a record." But they encouraged me.

For example, Black students at Kenwood and other public schools across the city held very organized system-wide Monday boycotts in October 1968. Many parents forbade their kids from participating, but my parents were supportive, in spite of some instances of retaliation. To discourage kids from boycotting, a lot of teachers would give big assignments that were due the day of the boycott, or they would give a test that day and wouldn't let you make it up. I remember my Latin teacher tried to give me a bad grade my second quarter, after I got an A or B first quarter. Then I went down to a D. My mother led the charge to stop teachers from punishing kids for boycotting.

Every Monday in October, we were out. More than thirty-five thousand kids boycotted their schools in support of more Black teachers and administrators, better materials and facilities, Black history courses and clubs. I will never forget those days. The boycotts were successful. The board of education caved on some things. There were changes in teaching faculty at some schools, an increase in the number of Black administrators, and new Black studies curricula at many schools.[3] For example, at Kenwood, we finally got a Black teacher to teach us Black history—we didn't call it African American history then.

But a big problem with the system-wide Black student movement was that the boys wanted to take front and center, even though the girls were actually doing more of the work. They used this misguided idea that Black families and communities were too matriarchal as the reason that Black men had been put down for so long, saying, "It's time for us to take a step forward." My question was, "Why can't we take the steps together?"

Mind you, I was fifteen, I wasn't dating, and I didn't understand this kind of male chauvinism. I didn't have any brothers and I was the first child, so my parents did not treat me like a girl, so to speak. I had no real thorough sex-role socialization. In my household, it wasn't that I did the dishes and all the inside work, I also had to do the yard work, take out the garbage, shovel snow, all the stuff that boys would normally do. I did all that because there were no brothers. So that left me in a very curious position when it came to dealing with boys and their egos. I didn't get it. While my parents could be uptight, our home was quite egalitarian in this way.

There was this guy Brother Omar, kind of a light-skinned dude with a big 'fro, like everybody had in those days. I remember him being at a meeting at the Umoja Center. The Umoja Black Student Center was a storefront on Thirty-Ninth Street in Bronzeville with pictures of Malcolm X and other Black revolutionaries on the window. It was the home base for the Afro-American Student Association. I was happy there was a space for Black students to meet close to home on the South Side. But at one meeting, Brother Omar basically told us that it was time for the sisters to step back and let the brothers come forward, and that we needed to be supporting the brothers by making bean pies in the kitchen while they ran the organization. That's what I remember. Why are you bringing this misogyny and this patriarchy here? So, we gon' be oppressed by brothers now, instead of white people? That wasn't going to work! Not only that, it was all the little socialist white girls with no bras on and no drawers on coming to other student organizing meetings that I attended. I remember them taking down their hair and letting it all fall, and the brothers are all drooling and whatnot. I remember that time being absolutely ridiculous.

We were serious, trying to figure out how to make the movement *work*, how to change things, and they were busy being fascinated by white P-U-S-S-Y they couldn't have. That's when I was done with the Black student movement in Chicago. First of all, I didn't know how to make bean pies. Second of all, I did not understand why we had to take a back seat. And nobody explained it to me well. When I brought it to my parents, they sat me down and tried to break it down and explain these dynamics to me. It made sense, but I didn't want to be a part of it.

Someone once asked me why the Black Panther movement fell apart. As I saw it, there were two reasons. First and foremost was COINTELPRO—the government's illegal counterintelligence program that surveilled, infiltrated, discredited, and destroyed many activist groups during this time. But the other reason was the ego of men. Even when I was in high school, I felt like I was a natural leader, and I didn't want any part of taking a back seat to Black men because I was a Black woman.

At the same time, I remember not feeling tied to the women's movement at all, watching and listening to white women talk about feminism. It seemed like the women's movement was for middle-class white women. I always thought that white women brought racism and white privilege to the table but never wanted to acknowledge it. They also wanted to spend a whole lot of time telling me about how I was oppressed when I wasn't experiencing oppression in the same ways. I was feeling oppression from being Black, not from being female. Because I was able to *push through* a lot of stuff. Because I had a father and a grandfather who made me feel worthy and loved me unconditionally. I'm a Black woman in America with all the double standards that come with it.

In 1969, Fred Hampton was assassinated by law enforcement officers as he slept in the apartment where he was staying with other members of the Black Panther Party. Officers also shot and killed Mark Clark in the raid that was coordinated by the Cook County State's Attorney's Office, the Chicago Police Department, and the FBI. When Fred Hampton was murdered, it changed a *whole* lot of people's trajectories. We *all* thought he was the embodiment of the movement. He'd championed free breakfast for children, free medical care, free busing to prisons, free ambulance service, and free clothing for people who couldn't afford it. What they started with free breakfast for children was something that the government looked at and copied! Fred and the Panthers were doing it on the West Side in the 1960s, and it took until the 2000s for CPS to see the value in free breakfast for all students. His murder frightened me. That somebody could just bust down your door and come in shooting while you were asleep? It frightened me to no end. I sort of took a respite from activism at that point, because I didn't really know *whose* list I was on.

Chapter 4

Freedom in the Happy Valley

Even when I was more engaged in activism, I was still a kid doing high school things. I was enjoying high school, to be honest. I didn't dislike it. Kenwood was a great school. Plus, I was a member of Kenwood's second entering class, and it was fun to be in a place where there were not really upperclassmen, and there was nobody oppressing you for being new and younger. There was nobody to sell you elevator passes and stuff like that. What was not to love? We got to set all the standards.

I was the editor of the school newspaper starting my freshman year. Since we were only in the second class, we didn't have anybody else to do it. Someone asked, "Well, who wants to do it?" and I said, "I'll do it." I mean, why not? We named the newspaper the *Kaleidoscope*. And I wrote the first column of the school year. They ran that column at the beginning of every school year for *years*. Being managing editor of your high school newspaper for three years was a pretty good gig, and it looks good on your resume. I also was in the math and computer club and was corresponding secretary in the student council.

But I decided to leave Kenwood High School after my junior year and go to Mount Holyoke College in South Hadley, Massachusetts. I was sixteen. It was one of the best decisions I made in my life. Back in the day, a lot of kids were starting college a year early; there was also a counselor pushing us to do this, encouraging us. The counselor's own daughter got into Wellesley after her junior year, and she had also gotten another kid into Yale, back when it was still all male. Some of the best schools offered that option. I didn't do anything special. I just took an achievement test and applied as if I was a senior during my junior year.

I was asking to go away to college a year early and I thought choosing a women's college would smooth the way with my parents. I knew there would be blowback. But I didn't know how *vicious* it would be coming from my mother. That's when I realized my mother had some strange issues. I knew that my father would go for Holyoke because my father had these delusions of grandeur about me. He wanted me to be Miss America, but he also wanted me to have a very solid liberal arts education. And then when he saw those girls skiing down hills in Massachusetts, he was all into that because we *loved* the Winter Olympics. My father and I excitedly watched Jean-Claude Killy sweep the downhill and slalom events at the 1968 Winter Olympics. I knew I could get my father to come around to me going to college if I went to Mount Holyoke—an all-women's school, and there was skiing. He loved it.

My father knew that it was an opportunity for his daughter, one that he and my mother had never had. I took him to all of my college interviews. Because I applied not only to Mount Holyoke, but also to all the Seven Sisters schools—except Barnard, Radcliffe, and Wellesley, which I decided was too close to Boston. I didn't want to be in a big city because I knew I would get distracted. Barnard was definitely out, because I knew I would be distracted by New York City! I had a love affair with New York from the time I was a little bitty kid. But I wanted a different experience for college. I wanted to be in the middle of nowhere.

My mother was not OK with it. I'd gotten into a petty argument with her, and she told me as punishment that I couldn't go to Mount Holyoke. I felt she just wanted to control me. For example, I'd already gotten into the University of Chicago, and she was overjoyed, but then I realized it was because that had been *her* college experience. She had not left home to go to college. She grew up in Saint Louis and she lived at home and went to Stowe Teachers College. She told me I wasn't ready to go yet. She hadn't taught me everything I needed to know in order to live. I was like, "I've had *enough*!"

When my mother said no, that I couldn't go to Mount Holyoke, it was the first time I remember my father standing up to her. He said, "Oh yeah, she's going. Yes, she's going." I checked my mom about that years later. "Oh, I only said that because of the finances." I said, "Mama, stop lying." Talk about revisionist history; she is a master at that.

I went to college in September of '70. Mount Holyoke is gorgeous, one of the prettiest campuses I've ever been on. It was like paradise—I felt *free*! Because it was away, it was in the hills. In the Pioneer Valley—what they called the part of Massachusetts where Mount Holyoke was—there were hills, forests, and beautiful trees and old houses. And mountains, which I had never really seen or paid attention to before. It was a reset. Who knew that a teenager could make great decisions, especially when we're told the frontal lobe of their young brains isn't fully formed (which apparently explains their aberrant behavior)? At sixteen, I made a decision that would provide me with access to the best academic institutions in America at a time when these institutions were looking to begin addressing centuries of a lack of diversity. Technically, I had the opportunity to utilize the tools of affirmative action to change the trajectory of my life.

There are five liberal arts colleges tucked away in Western Massachusetts—the Happy Valley, as it's still called today—and Mount Holyoke is part of the Five College Consortium, which also includes Amherst, Hampshire, the University of Massachusetts Amherst, and Smith. Someone compared the Five Colleges to *Scooby-Doo* for me. Shaggy is Hampshire. Velma is Mount Holyoke: smart as hell, but frumpy. Daphne is Smith. Fred is Amherst—with the ascot. And Scooby was UMass. That one I don't get. I thought UMass actually had better professors. They had more *interesting* professors. They had a music program at UMass, where jazz drummer Max Roach taught. Amherst College had Professor Asa Davis as the first director of Black Studies up there. Happy Valley was just pretty amazing. What a place to come of age . . . and it's so *beautiful*. In the fall, oh my gosh. You don't want to be anywhere else.

A Mount Holyoke girl is—*I* think—very bright but very down-to-earth. Smithies are bright, but they're kind of bougie. They have more money. And especially the Black ones. I think it probably is that way with the white girls too. Then there's Hampshire, which was just getting started when I was there in 1970. Hampshire is more *freeee spiriiiit*. All of the professors were high. It wasn't just us. And then UMass was *cool* because UMass had brothers from the hood. When I was there, Julius Erving—Dr. J—was playing basketball there. I got to see him do some amazing things. And I kept telling people about this guy. I said, "Wait until you see him, this brother from New York. You have never seen *aaanything* like this." And everyone would say, "*Yeah* . . . Connie Hawkins." "Yeah, you're right. Connie Hawkins. But you ain't seen *nothing* until you see Dr. J!" And he was very *nice*! That's the other thing about him. He was very nice and very accessible.

Mount Holyoke was academically rigorous and purposely nurturing. It was so affirming to be at an all-women's school, where everyone was focused on learning and being accomplished. It was like being in a Jane Austen novel or something. You would sit at the dinner table and you would talk about what you were reading or what you were thinking about, not just dates and diets. It was so different from high school.

And at Holyoke we ran all over. Over to Amherst and to UMass. There were three of us that came out of Kenwood and went to the Yoke. Two of us were from the junior class and the other one was a class ahead of us. She went as a senior, like normal people. But we all came in together the same year because of that. This was thanks to the Kenwood counselor facilitating all of it. It was a strong cohort in a school of thirteen hundred.

At Holyoke, the girls I was pretty close with were Black girls who lived on the "boots and saddles" side of the third floor at Ham Hall, right by Lower Lake. I lived in the language dorm, on the Italian side of the floor. Joyce Bohannon and Vanessa Hickey were from Atlanta, and they were *good* Southern girls, very ladylike. I really didn't get them at first it took me a while to understand them. But eventually they won me over—they were *so* nice! However, the Southern girls liked going to the Westover Air Force base. I never cared for the Air Force boys—I was not interested in servicemen.

I also took different classes from some of the other girls I ran with. They were looking forward to going to law school. I was majoring in music and sociology and taking Italian as my language requirement. One of my best friends was my freshman year roommate, Peggy Kidney; I lived with her on the Italian floor, and she now lives in Italy. I loved Italian opera so much that I wanted to conduct—I figured I'd be the first Black woman to do it. But it was too much work! I was having too much fun. And you've got to practice if you want to be a music major. I often ditched classes, even the most interesting ones, because I liked to sleep late. I didn't want to sign up for any early classes. The earliest class I ever took met at nine o'clock. I majored in *graduation*, is what I'd tell people. "Graduation, sleep, and bid whist."

§

I hitchhiked with my friend to Dartmouth from Mount Holyoke. We got a ride to Putney, Vermont, with John Irving, who wrote the book *The World According to Garp*. Putney wasn't that far from where we lived in Massachusetts. Irving said, "Well, girls, this is as far as I'm going. Good luck." He let us out on Interstate 91, about sixty miles away from Dartmouth's campus in Hanover. That's the way it was in the old days. When you hitchhiked, you went as far as the driver was going. He was turning off 91 and going into Putney, so it wouldn't have made sense for him to bring us into Putney. I think it took us two more rides to get to Dartmouth, but it was fun. I thought hitchhiking was the way to go. I didn't know you were supposed to take trains and buses and stuff. My parents used to tell me that hitchhiking was dangerous. It just didn't feel that way back then. And I think, at that age, you're in the upside of your risk-taking years. We were still surrounded by this environment that felt very protective and nurturing.

Going to Mount Holyoke shifted my orientation to white people. I remember reading those Falconhurst books about slavery, like *Mandingo* and *Drum*, in the sixties. The books were filled with graphic scenes of violence on the fictional Falconhurst plantation. They were popular "slave fiction," not historical texts.[1] And they were different than anything I had ever read about slavery. I was like, "Oh my God!" It made me understand slavery in a way that I hadn't understood it before. I hadn't realized that slavery was so *emotionally* brutal. I knew you got beat under slavery. But I did not realize that families had been torn apart or that your father could actually be your master and then would watch you get beat; I didn't understand the intimacy and emotional terror of that. And that knowledge made me angry for a while. But being at Mount Holyoke kind of tempered that for me. It changed how I saw white people. It's weird because when I went to Kenwood, there were some white students, and it was more racially diverse than most CPS schools. Kenwood was intentionally created to keep white kids and middle-class Black kids in the public school system. But Holyoke was still my first time in a majority white educational space. I still knew racism was alive and well. I grew my hair out into a big Angela Davis Afro. I thought she was a goddess. She was so inspiring. And I participated in Black student organizing at Holyoke. But at Holyoke, more than before, I started to see white people as real human beings.

I transferred after two years at the Yoke and ended up graduating from Dartmouth. I made the decision to transfer there because of a boyfriend and because Dartmouth was about to become a coed institution. They didn't want just a freshman setup—they wanted girls in all the other classes too. So, for the junior and senior classes, they invited young women applicants who'd participated in things like the Twelve-College Exchange

Program, a domestic study abroad program where students attended a different college for a semester or for a year. I hadn't done that program, but I was close to a guy from Dartmouth because he was dating one of my girlfriends, Kathleen, whom I was close to at Mount Holyoke. So I had visited Dartmouth before.

When *Dartmouth Alumni Magazine* interviewed me in 2011, I let them know how terrible my time in the college was, and they published those quotes!

> Dartmouth was a really bad experience for me, but it made me stronger. I was the only Black woman in my class, and it was clear that women weren't wanted. That did teach me that top-down decisions usually take a while for people to buy into. When I came back to campus with my husband John he wondered if I'd really gone to Dartmouth, because I didn't know my way around very well. I'd spent my time pretty much hunkered down.

Chicago Magazine printed a similar quote, when a journalist asked me what I majored in at Dartmouth:

> I always say graduation. I don't really remember Dartmouth that well. It was a really awful experience. I'm the only Black woman in my class. So it was like being a complete and total pioneer. . . . I barely graduated. . . . I changed my major about every fifteen minutes. But Dartmouth was an interesting experience. It just taught me that you have to persevere. . . . People did not want us there. The faculty and the students did not vote for coeducation; the trustees did, so there was a lot of hostility toward us.[2]

When people hear that I went to Dartmouth and was the only Black woman in my graduating class, they are always impressed, but I spent those years smoking lots of weed—self-medicating. Dartmouth was tough, but it was truly a learning experience.

I took these lessons about the failures of top-down decision-making with me. And I got out of there and went to Oklahoma.

Chapter 5

Something to Do, Someone to Love, Something to Look Forward To

I don't care what anyone says—my first marriage was *arranged*. And the matchmakers were my maternal grandmother and, in particular, my Aunt Mattie C.

My senior year at Dartmouth, I spent fall term with my paternal grandparents—Muddy and Popeye—in Muskogee, Oklahoma. My grandparents had moved back to Oklahoma from Chicago after my grandmother's twin sister, Aunt Maurene, died. Muddy didn't have any other close family left other than her youngest sister, my great-aunt, Mattie C., who lived in Muskogee. So they moved because Muddy wanted to be near her baby sister; matter of fact, they bought the house right behind Aunt Mattie C.'s house. Mattie C.'s house was on one street, and my grandmother's house was right behind hers on the next street over. Popeye and Muddy were at the ages when their friends and family members were dying, and much of their social lives focused on church or funerals. At age twenty, I chose to pass on both.

But one day, my grandmother came home with a special lilt in her voice, saying, "You should have come to the funeral. You would have met Arnold Leo." I thought going to a funeral would be a terrible place to meet someone. "Who's Arnold Leo?" I asked. "Legs's boy," she countered. "Legs?" I was confused. Legs and my grandmother grew up together in Taft, Oklahoma, a really small Black town. Since Legs was my grandmother's friend from childhood, I figured "Legs's boy" must have been my father's age. They kept wanting me to meet him and I'm like, "*Legs's* boy? He must be forty, fifty years old!" But Muddy assured me that Legs had married a significantly younger woman, Sarah.

Now Legs himself was a very dapper gentleman. I never saw him without a three-piece suit, even though he had been retired for years. I don't care where he was going, if he was sitting in his house all day, Legs had a three-piece suit on and a tie, and he was always *cleaaan*. Clean, clean, clean.

At any rate, the next week we were off to Kansas City for yet another funeral. I declined that invitation and spent the afternoon with my Aunt Velma's son, Buster, who had come from Saint Louis.

We spent a lot of summers in Saint Louis, so the last time I had seen Buster was my sixteenth birthday in 1969. That birthday was sidelined because Neil Armstrong decided to land on the moon, and no one paid attention to me. I thought Buster was racially confused, and that summer, he spent an inordinate amount of time asking me why I wore my hair in an Afro. Why I embraced my Negritude. I didn't understand him, but he was clear about the fact that he presented himself as Portuguese. It didn't dawn on me until years later that Buster must have suffered under Jim Crow. Instead of expressing that outwardly, I think he turned it in on himself by denying the Black part of his life.

Uncle Harry, Buster's father and namesake, was from New Bedford, Massachusetts, which has a large Portuguese population, but Uncle Harry was dark (and very handsome), and I could easily see how Aunt Velma fell in love with him. Uncle Harry's family is from the Cape Verde islands off the coast of Africa. Cape Verde was a Portuguese colony. When Buster said he was Portuguese or told me he didn't know what he was, I would say, "Well, what about your mother? I'll tell you what she is—she's my mama's sister, and my mama's *Black*! Then you're Black. This is America, and there's the one-drop rule."

You know, looking in the mirror, all I ever saw was Black. I *never* understood this color shit. It didn't make any sense to me, especially as a kid. I thought a lot of white people were Black because they were married to Black people. When I was young, I didn't realize there was interracial marriage. But two of my best friends, Barry and Bradley, their mother was white. And I didn't know it for *years*! I just thought she was Black! Who knew? I also remember when I learned that my aunt Dorothy was white. When I was about six years old coming home from school, somebody said, "Your mama's a Black bitch." It was really hurtful. I talked to my mother about it, and she said, "Well, we don't say things like that. We certainly don't use color to differentiate. I would never say Aunt Dorothy's a *white* bitch." I looked at her and I said, "*What?!* Aunt Dorothy's not Black?" "No." "Not a Negro?" "No." "*What?!*" It really confused me for a *long* time.

Other than my cousin Buster, who I think passed at some point, my family was pretty unified when it came to race. I even asked my mother directly about why she chose not to pass. She had been talking about how, in the Jim Crow days, they couldn't go sit in the same part in the theaters—they had to sit in the balcony. And I said, "Well, why didn't you pass?" Do you know what she said to me? "Because it was against the law." They were raised to be "correct." And they were part of the Black community in Saint Louis, which was important to them.

People make the assumption that I'm biracial. White mothers come up to me, presuming I'm biracial, and ask me for advice about their biracial children. I have to respond, "I can't help you, I'm not biracial. I don't *know* that." Other people think I'm Creole. But I'm not from Louisiana and I'm not Creole. Some people also think I'm Latina. Every time I go to New York, people start speaking Spanish to me. I've also met a lot of white people who think I'm white, and I don't get that either! As a matter of fact, people have looked at my husband and me and thought he was dating some white woman or something. And they'd snarl at us. I'd be confused, but my husband would explain, "They think you're white." And I'd say, "How?! There's nothing white about me!" I don't talk like a white woman. I don't act like a white woman. I'm just confused at how people would think that I was white. Especially with my hair. And when I wore dreadlocks, I really didn't understand it.

I've been asked if I've ever been with a white man. And I say, "Hell, no. For what?" White men aren't interested in me. They don't get any cred for being with someone who looks like me. If they date Black women, white men usually like darker brown women so that people will notice and say, "Oh, look. Look what he's doing." They don't get points for me.

Anyway, back to the story about hanging out with Buster in Oklahoma. At a certain point, I had second thoughts about not attending the funeral. Mercifully, my grandparents got back, and my grandmother was cheery as all get-out when I got in the car. "You should have been to the funeral. Arnold Leo was there!" I finally looked at her and asked intently, "Why is this guy going to all these funerals?" She looked at me like I was a six-year-old. "That's because all his people are dying." Made sense, and I tossed it in the back of my head.

One Saturday, my grandparents and my great-aunt, Mattie C., packed us all up to take our show on the road to Tulsa, to visit relatives. We ended up at our cousin Cleo's house. Unbeknownst to me, Aunt Mattie C., because she was the one playing matchmaker, called Arnold Leo and told him to come over. She came into the room with a Cheshire grin and announced, "I've got a surprise for you." About two hours later, the doorbell rang. In walked one of the sexiest men I had ever seen in my life. It was Legs's boy—Arnold Leo Glenn. Then he spoke: the most velvety, mellifluous, bass-baritone tones. Think dark-chocolate truffles with merlot, dimples, deep-brown eyes, and gleaming white teeth. Not to mention six foot three, 230 pounds. I *swear* I heard love songs in the back of my head, you know? I was through. I wish I *had* met him earlier! Just everything I could ever dream about in a man—that's who he was.

All my friends said he looked like a "chocolate Stacy Keach." I never thought Stacy Keach was particularly good-looking or anything, but my husband, Glenn—that's what I called him—had big brown eyes, just like my current husband, John, and a dimple, just like John.

Glenn invited me to his house. "I'm having some people over, we're playing cards. Would you like to come?" I wanted to go, but my grandparents were ready to head back to Muskogee, so I politely declined. We agreed to try to catch up with each other at a later date, but I didn't think much would come of it. Boy, was I ever wrong.

When we finally agreed upon a time to meet, he stood me up! He was two hours late, then he finally called, only to cancel the date! I was really mad about it. So I said, "Well, why are you canceling?" He said, "Well, I got something I gotta do," blah blah blah. "Well, why can't you still come?" He said OK, but he never showed. That taught me a *really* good lesson: Listen to what men say. Because when they tell you something, that's what they mean. He said he wasn't coming, but I wanted to hear something else so I didn't pay any attention, and then he didn't come. I still thought he was fine as hell, so I was just like, "OK, I have to put up with this bullshit." I was bored to death sitting around my grandparents' house in Muskogee, so I let Glenn whisk me off to Tulsa.

This was October of 1973, and by April 1974, he had given me an engagement ring and asked me to marry him. I said yes. He had a ring, you know? Whirlwind and arranged. My college graduation was on June 9 and we got married on June 15. I basically had no plans after graduation. I was twenty years old and Glenn was twenty-six. Maybe not the best decision, but at that time and place, the best one for me.

It made my parents happy because they decided it meant I wasn't a ho. My grandma was happy as hell because the families had known each other for years. At one point, his uncle had been engaged to my great-aunt, one of my grandmother's sisters. For her, it was like the Bakers and the Glenns were back together. I think there's something to be said about those kinds of marriages because you know who your kids are, and they know who their kids are—they had worked together.

§

I lived in Tulsa for most of the '70s and it was a real challenge for me to be there. After Chicago and the Happy Valley, it was a massive cultural change; I felt no intellectual stimulation or engagement whatsoever. I also found Okies to be some of the most scared people I've ever met in my life. It was that hushed "Get *out* of here, talking about that *freedom* stuff. *Shhhhhh.* You're going to get us *all* killed." When I was in Oklahoma in the '70s, I felt like the '60s had never touched the place. We were fifteen years behind the rest of the country!

For one thing, the 1921 Tulsa Massacre scarred Black folks; when I was living there, people still talked about it. And when Black Wall Street—the Black Greenwood community in Tulsa—was devastated, the only thing left, surprisingly, was the newspaper. I worked for that newspaper for a while. By that time, it had passed down to the youngest son. I sold advertising and I worked for this old guy who had been with the paper for forty or fifty years. He was a character. He had *plenty* of stories. He asked, "Who are your people?" So I told him about my grandfather Popeye, who I think drove the Pine Street bus in the city. Pine Street crossed Greenwood Avenue, which ran through the heart of the Greenwood community that was attacked during the massacre. Black Wall Street included Greenwood, Archer, and Pine Streets—that's where The Gap Band gets its name from.

I also found the white people in Tulsa extraordinarily and overtly racist. I worked at American Airlines for about two and a half years as a computer programmer. One day my boss said to me, "Oh, have you met the other colored fellow that we just hired?" I didn't understand why, in 1977, he was using the word *colored*. I mean, I personally like the word, but that doesn't give white folks the right to use it. So I said, "Colored fellow? What color is he?" Some guy replied, "Oh, he's Black." I said, "Oh. No, I haven't met him yet." He turned out to be a really nice guy. We were all programmers together. I hated writing code. It was the most boring job I ever had.

I had lots of different jobs in Tulsa. My first job after I got married was as a counselor at a drug rehab center. I didn't have any experience as a counselor, but since I had a sociology degree they figured I could do it. I enjoyed that job, but I got tired of it because drug addiction is so deep, and it was hard when it felt like I couldn't help people really heal. I also worked at a place for unwed mothers, helping connect them with supports they were entitled to—WIC benefits, job training, clothes for interviews. Before Glenn became a firefighter, he had worked in real estate with his uncle, who had a real estate firm. They tried to get me to go into real estate. I had no interest in it, but I loved going to school, so I did take a real estate class. I learned the whole nature of how mortgages really work, how you calculate one, how you calculate the value of a property, how you get comps, and other stuff. But it wasn't the job for me. I preferred my part-time job answering the phone for things like Ginsu knives and the *Wall Street Journal.* That was one of my favorite jobs I ever had. The only job that came anywhere close to that was teaching. Ginsu knives and teaching. Go figure!

While some folks were venturing out to Tulsa's south side in the '70s, most Black people lived on the north side of town where Glenn and I lived. The beautiful thing about the north side was that there were *all* kinds of neighborhoods there, class-wise. I think that segregation does have advantages sometimes; you could live right next door to a doctor or a lawyer, but a few blocks away from Skillet and Bubba. At the time, there wasn't any real Black politics at the city level. The mayor and all his cronies were white, and I remember very few Black politicians.

One of the problems I had living in Oklahoma was all these white people who thought I was white. I had a white coworker named Dusty at American Airlines. Her son, she told me, had complained about me. He said to her, "You know, I don't like white people that act Black." And so she said, "Uh, Karen's Black." Oh, so *then* it was OK that I could be myself.

There was also this old man at the place where I used to play tennis. My husband was playing tennis one day, but my partner hadn't shown up yet. This little old white man who I saw every day was there—I always spoke to him on the tennis court. That day he said, "You're not a n****r lover, are you?" "*What* did you say?! Obviously, I am, old man." And he said it again! So I said, "Yes, I am! Not only that, I'm a n***a too!" Guess who never sat next to *me* anymore.

There wasn't much to do in my new hometown, and I was crazy about my husband, so the early days of our marriage were a whole lot of sex, drugs, and rock and roll. Which was not bad! But I didn't know what I wanted. I was twenty and bored out of my mind, so I tried to find interesting things to do. When Glenn became a firefighter, it was definitely a good thing, because every three days, I had a whole twenty-four hours to myself. I would go to the opera, the ballet, or do stuff I knew he wouldn't want to do.

But while we had some different interests, my husband was smart as shit. He read all the time. We were intellectually matched. And we would have these wonderful, interesting discussions. He once told me, "You better know your enemics. Read *Atlas Shrugged*." That book by Ayn Rand. I had my doubts, but I read it and I learned a lot from that book. I learned that there were people out there who felt like if you didn't work, you shouldn't eat. And that those people were alive and well, taking up airspace, and really serious. They always think they did everything themselves, that they got nothing handed to them, when every last one of them got something handed to them. If you don't understand what your enemy has planned for you, then you can't have a counterplan. That's a lesson I've taken with me through my whole life. And because of that, it's one of my favorite books. Glenn put me on to that.

My husband was very bright, but he didn't finish college. He had attended Philander Smith, later transferred to University of Arkansas Pine Bluff, and was eight credit hours shy of graduating. I remember one of my mother-in-law's friends saying, "Well, why wouldn't you just send him back there and let him do a day and he'll be done?" not understanding the process or how credit hours were calculated.

Nevertheless, Glenn grew me up. I was *pretty* dang naïve, I think. On our first date, he took me to a little bar in a strip mall—I had never seen nor heard of a bar in a strip mall before. When we got there, my husband was paying the cover charge. He bent down and some woman grabbed him. I didn't know what to think! I finally asked him, "Did you know her?" Because he got up, turned, and looked at her like she was crazy. He said no. I said, "Oh, so the women here just grab what they want, huh?" And I thought that was funny as hell.

I've never been jealous. I've always felt like your man—whoever he is—has chosen you, when he had the opportunity to choose other women and didn't. So, in my mind, I'd already won. My husband had been on the dating scene for a while because he was older than me, so as far as I was concerned, he had a choice. Even his mother told him that I was the best thing that would ever happen to him: "I told him, you're a baby. He's gotta be careful with you." But I don't think he really understood what that meant. Once, he said something mean to me, and I called my mother-in-law in tears. She said, "He said *what*?" And I said, "Yeah!" I mean, I never argued like that before with any of my boyfriends. We never called each other names. She told me, "Don't pay attention to that fool," but she used the N-word.

I learned a lot from Glenn. He taught me that the people you work with aren't necessarily your friends. He taught me how to read between the lines. He gave me all the street smarts that I think I have now—I learned all that from Glenn. He could be brutal sometimes, emotionally. He would just go for the jugular, and I learned how to fight with him. He taught me how to hit below the belt with my words. I didn't necessarily think that was ethical, but I think it was still good to have learned that, even though I don't think you should use it with people you love. I've also learned, since I've gotten older, how *not* to fight. But think about it: he was twenty-six, I was twenty. And he was a *spectacular* human being—he was sexy, he was wonderful. And I was *so* in love with him. I would just take one look at him and swoon. Yet he was hard! He was a challenge.

One challenge was that Glenn was very impatient, partially because he always believed he was going to die young. He said to me, "I'm gonna ask you to marry me. But I'm gonna tell you what—I'm not going to live to see forty-seven." He had that sense because he had high blood pressure from the time he was sixteen years old. And he was living a kind of fast, burn-it-down life. So from the time we met, he'd always said, "I'm not gonna live that long."

He was always honest with me. He said, "I don't want children because I'll never live to see them grown, and I don't want to burden you with trying to raise children by yourself." I wasn't that sold on kids for a variety of reasons. For one thing, I knew I didn't want a boy because I don't know anything about boys. How do you raise a Black son if you don't have brothers? You don't know the ideology of boys. And then I was just too afraid, in this society . . . I mean, *terribly* fearful. I never thought that anybody could get to *me*, but they could get to me through my children because that's how you're vulnerable. That's how I felt.

Believe it or not, I got that theory from those books by Carlos Castañeda, including *The Teachings of Don Juan*. Don Juan is like a wizard—a kind of medicine man, spiritualist, whatever he is—and Carlos goes to study with him and, I mean, this guy appears out of nowhere, in the Sonoran Desert. And he tells Carlos, "You have two children"—or something like that, I don't remember exactly—and Carlos says, "How do you know that?" And Don Juan says, "Because there are two holes in your being, and that's where your children are. And that's how the world gets to you, through your child." Reading that, I thought, "Oh my, that's so true!" I absorbed that message.

I don't have children—and that's deliberate. I didn't want to fuck 'em up. I saw all my friends that had kids, and their kids were really messed up. I didn't feel like I had the skill set for parenting, especially with a husband who didn't want children. Why would you bring kids into the world when you know that doesn't work for you?

There was one time when I wanted to have a baby. Glenn had said to me, "OK, when you're twenty-seven, we can revisit this issue." So when I turned twenty-seven, I raised it again. And he was like, "Ehh . . ."

And that's when he told me that I had outgrown him. He said, "You know, it's time for you to go. You've outgrown me." I thought it was a really deep thing to say. How do you tell somebody, "You've outgrown me?" Can you imagine saying that to your wife? I don't even know what to say about it, except that he was extraordinary. I didn't want to go, but I knew it was time. It was weird. I knew he was right! He had been right about everything else, so why would he be wrong about this?

We stayed friends. We were in constant contact. Matter of fact, I had left Tulsa, but he was supposed to come and visit me. We got our schedules tweaked, incorrectly. And he said, "Well, I'll just have to do it next year." The following year, I hadn't heard from Glenn so I made plans with this guy I was dating in DC. Then I finally heard from him, and I was like, "Man, I already made plans." So we decided that the next year—1989—we would get together in August. But he died on March 31, 1989.

When he died, it was *awful.* He was forty-one; I was thirty-five. He died on a Friday night, and I got the phone call Saturday morning from my girlfriend who still lived in Tulsa. She said, "Are you sitting down?" I said, "You just woke me up, so I'm on the toilet. Yes. I'm sitting down." She said, "Girl, our Glenn died." At first, I was thinking it must be my father-in-law. When I asked, she said, "It's your husband." It was horrible. I don't even have words for it. I don't know how to describe that feeling. It was a huge loss for me for a very long time.

First of all, I felt really guilty. I kept feeling that had I been *with* him, I could have monitored him better. I also felt like the only person in the world who *knew* me, understood me, and loved me—in spite of it—was gone. My guilt lasted a good long time. I had to work through it in therapy. It was just painful, extremely painful. And then, six weeks later, my father-in-law died. I shifted to feeling bad for my mother-in-law, who had buried her son and her husband in the span of six weeks. When I asked her, "Sarah, how did you make it through that?" she told me, "God." I guess I got that, but I was going through my atheist phase at the time, and it seemed so unfair. I would have these dreams about

Glenn for the longest time. It was hard for me to believe he was gone! Permanently.

He was such a brilliant person. He would say, "You only need three things in this world: You need something to do, someone to love, and something to look forward to." I thought that was wise and I still believe it to be true.

Chapter 6

Finding Teaching

After my husband and I separated, I came home to Chicago. I moved in temporarily with my mother, who still lived there. She kept saying, “Get your sub certificate. Get your sub certificate.” She wanted me to be a teacher. But I wouldn’t do it. When I came home, one of my friends was running a camp program at Elmhurst College in the suburbs of Chicago, in conjunction with the NFL Players Association, to expose Black and Brown kids to certain professions. And it wasn’t just medicine or law. She invited butchers, undertakers, and firefighters. Speakers were featured in the morning, and in the afternoon, the kids ran their own little city, with a grocery store, a newspaper, and a police department. They were so funny and smart!

I went out to the camp to help my friend, but I still hadn’t decided my next moves. I was trying to write a book, and my friend from high school asked me to visit and talk to the kids about being a writer. Then the lead counselor who ran the newspaper at the camp left in the middle of the program. My friend knew I’d been the editor-in-chief of the *Kaleidoscope*, our high school newspaper at Kenwood, for three years, so she asked if I would take over. For a while, I did that.

Remarkably, there was a well-connected guy from Barbados at the camp, checking it out. After sitting in on my class, he invited me to come back with him and start a camp down there. I agreed.

For some reason, I'd wanted to live in Barbados my entire life. I don't know what it was, but I heard that name when I was a kid and said to myself: "I want to live there. It's in the tropics. It's Black people." But they used to call it Little England, which was striking. While I lived in Barbados, I became very anticolonial. But Barbados was *certainly* not the place to be for that. For example, unlike a lot of people there, I didn't watch Diana and Prince Charles's 1981 wedding. I had gotten a ride with some guy—because you can hitchhike all over Barbados—and he asked if I would be getting up for the royal wedding. I said, "No, I will not. I'm an American. We got rid of that. In 1776."

I ended up living in Barbados for a year and I wanted to continue living there. The people were so nice. There was this one family that just took me *in*. My best memories of Barbados are of the people. And it was just a beautiful place. But I couldn't get a job because if you're not a Bajan (native to Barbados), you can't get a job that a Bajan can do. I asked what kinds of jobs they needed. When they said, "We need physicians," I said, "OK, I'll go to medical school."

I applied to medical school at the University of Illinois in Chicago and was admitted. I returned to Chicago, started medical school, and soon flunked out. People were shocked that I left medical school. But I hated it. I fucking hated it. Why would I struggle with something that I really wasn't called to do? I do think I'd have been fine, and I would have made the best out of it, but it wasn't for me. I decided then to get my teaching credentials to see if I could teach chemistry.

I had moved back in with my mother when I was in medical school. It wasn't easy. She thought she would get to teach me the things she didn't get a chance to teach me before. I looked at her with a straight face and I said, "Ma, it's too late for that." Really, there wasn't much she *could* teach me. I had been married—grown and married. I just said, "You don't know anything about relationships. How you gon' help me? *You* project *your* things onto other people." I had watched her do that my whole life and it was always kind of a train wreck. So in a way I felt sorry for her, and in another way, she was smothering me.

But the best part of moving back home and my medical school experience was meeting my very best friend, Ann Sarpy, on the first day of medical school. She's a psychiatrist now, and one of the funniest dames I've ever met in my life. She had this long blond hair. When I saw her hanging out with these Black guys, I thought, "What is that white girl doing with all these bro-skis?" Then she turned around and I saw her face and her features, and I knew she was Black. But that blond hair had me. I saw her, and I just fell out laughing right then. From that moment, we started hanging out.

We'll get together and just talk smack. And giggle! Because you need to giggle on the regular. Her daughter, Samantha, is my goddaughter. I'll never forget how she looked up at me and opened her eyes on the first day she got here. I was holding her. And I just burst into tears. Because I knew I was going to be her godmother. Ann told me, "I just know you will always do the best for my daughter." I said, "You are absolutely right."

In an unexpected way, medical school also prepared me for organizing and politics. I wanted to make sure people understood what was really going on behind the closed doors. I mean, it's the sausage-making. I think going through anatomy in medical school, where you are cutting up cadavers and looking at stuff, if you can't stand it, you'll *never* make it through if you ain't ready for that. Now, that part I didn't mind at *all.*

§

I've always felt comfortable in my own skin. I've always had confidence. I've always felt like any job I ever wanted, any school I ever wanted to go to, I could get in. I could get the job I wanted. But I'm still not a big fan of work—you have to do it. So you've got to find something you love doing or you're going to be miserable. Finding teaching was the best thing for me because I had bounced from job to job to job before I entered the profession. I didn't stay on many jobs longer than six months—until I started teaching. I *loved* teaching.

I subbed for a year, but while I was subbing, I was taking education classes in the evening. After I completed that coursework, the only things I had left to do were methods and student teaching. At that time, a consortium of schools offered student teaching opportunities that could be taken in the summer; you didn't have to lose money if you were already working in schools. I went to Chicago State, which was the old Chicago Teachers College (CTC). So many Black teachers went through CTC. My husband John's older sister, Clara, went to CTC and became a teacher in the 1960s. For Black people in Chicago, it was *the* pathway into the profession. I took my secondary methods class at Chicago State and did my student teaching via the summer student teaching program. I did my student teaching at Kenwood when my father taught there.

Both my parents had significant teaching careers. My mother started teaching when I was about nine. I watched her go in and out of the workforce, as the family needs dictated. She stopped working at Spiegel to stay home with me when I was about seven because I was out of control, bouncing off the walls and stuff. My mother taught elementary school at Reavis—the same school I first attended. But she didn't start teaching there until 1962, after I got kicked out and sent to Kozminski. She left for maternity leave when my sister, Keli, was born, but otherwise stayed at Reavis until I went to college. When I went to college, she took some time off because financial aid was based on your income. She told me years later, "If I knew you were going to teach school, I'd have sent you to CTC instead of spending all that money to send you off to Holyoke."

My father left working in manufacturing and started teaching in 1963, the year my sister was born. I was ten. More schools had started opening up to Black students and Black teachers then because a lot of white kids were leaving the system. My father got a job at Parker High School on Sixty-Eighth and Stewart in Englewood. But it wasn't easy for him to become a certified teacher. I remember both my parents studying for the Chicago Teachers' Exam to get certified to teach in CPS, which at the time was really hard. The Chicago Teachers' Exam was required in addition to whatever the exam was for the state of Illinois, and everyone said it was harder than the state exam. There were three parts to the certification exam in Chicago: there was a written part, there was a practical part, and then there was an oral. You had to speak "standard English." The oral is what killed people. It was racist. They used the oral as a gatekeeping mechanism to deny Black people certification.

My dad whizzed through the practical section. He taught woodshop, so he made something beautiful. For the elementary school teachers, they had to teach a lesson. My father said that they would never pass Black male teachers to teach high school because, as he told it, "They didn't want them around young white girls." That was his take on it. He struggled to pass the exam and had to take it more than once before he passed. That test kept a *whooole* lot of Black people out of teaching or left them in the more precarious full-time substitute status with less pay.

When it was time for me to do my student teaching in the summer of 1987, my father was well over two decades into his teaching career and approaching retirement. He had left Parker years earlier, and he was teaching at Kenwood. One of his friends was an assistant principal at Kenwood, and I asked them if I could teach summer school chemistry. They hadn't planned to offer chemistry, but they said, "For you, we'll do it." And they did. They recruited a chemistry teacher, a Black man, probably in his late forties or early fifties, to teach at Kenwood that summer; I was able to do my student teaching with him. Starting that fall, I subbed for a year in elementary schools. They wouldn't let me teach high school—I don't know why because elementary school is so much harder—but a year later, in 1988, I got my first full-time teaching job at Sullivan High School.

§

My first year as a teacher, I spent a lot of time talking to the other teachers, asking—*begging*—for help. All I knew was, I didn't want to damage any of my children because I didn't know what the hell I was doing. For one thing, I didn't want to harm their self-esteem. And sometimes I did so by mistake. It's going to happen, but I learned that you have to forgive yourself.

Sullivan was amazing. At the time, I lived on Fifty-Fifth and Everett in Hyde Park and I was commuting to Sullivan in Rogers Park way up on the North Side. I taught on the North Side for years, but I never lived up there. It was an easy commute because it was straight up Lake Shore Drive. And it was beautiful because the lake is so gorgeous and changes every single day. For me, going up Lake Shore Drive to teach at Sullivan was all right!

I taught at Sullivan from 1988 to 1991. At the time, the school was very integrated for CPS and was led by a Black principal, Dr. Robert Brazil. Sullivan's students were about 50 percent Black, 27 percent Latinx, 11 percent Asian American and Pacific Islander, and 11 percent white. The families of Sullivan students came from many different countries and spoke several dozen different languages. The school had a faculty of about ninety teachers, but only about a quarter of the teachers were Black.[1] My primary mentors at Sullivan were white teachers and one Puerto Rican teacher. We were a tight group. We would go out drinking on Friday nights, and we always talked about how we could get better at our jobs. We talked about school and how to reach the kids who were struggling the most. It was a small and nurturing community for me, perfect for a new teacher.

I remember thinking that medical school had really prepared me for my work as a teacher. In med school, we learned Socratically, so I taught Socratically. And I was thankful to be in a place where I *could* teach Socratically. Sullivan's principal, Dr. Brazil, was a champion of the Paideia program, which included Socratic seminars and the great books. Sullivan was one of four schools in CPS that piloted the Paideia program, starting in 1984.[2] In the history and English classes, there were weekly seminars centering deep discussions about challenging readings. Once a quarter, we had an all-school seminar. In science and math, we ran quarterly seminars. Instead of reading the textbook about Boyle's law, we actually read what Boyle wrote. I later read an article in some magazine—it might have been *Science* magazine—where it turned out, Boyle's *wife* was doing all of his experiments. She was the one actually carrying them out while he was sitting there writing about it. So we *should* be calling it *Mrs.* Boyle's law. But I didn't know that when I was teaching it. Still, with the Paideia program at Sullivan, we embraced the notion of using primary sources, which I thought was wonderful. I wish this approach was offered in every school in the city. I felt like I was back at Mount Holyoke and Dartmouth. It was like being at a small liberal arts college.

All kids in high school have opinions, and our students were brilliant. In our Socratic seminars, you just couldn't spout opinions without going to the text and finding evidence. The kids at Sullivan impressed me; they seemed smarter than the kids I taught later at Lane Tech High School. Lane Tech had a long-standing reputation as a rigorous school. And Lane kids were solid performers, but Sullivan students were thinkers.

I taught at Sullivan for three years. But as a CPS teacher, I quickly found out that when you're competent, no good deed goes unpunished. It was decided that a Paideia prep program for seventh and eighth graders would be offered at Sullivan. The woman who'd been teaching it was the other chemistry teacher, and while she was sweet as all get-out, her classroom management skills were not cut out for younger kids. I don't know why exactly, but I had great classroom management skills. While I was a new teacher, I was in my mid-thirties when I started teaching—I already had real-life experience. I think this had something to do with it.

I also think many people don't realize how *hard* teachers have to work. It's not just standing in the front of the room imparting information. No. You have to do it in such slick ways that kids almost don't know they're being educated. Especially *now* because kids are so addicted to technology. I would always tell them, "Look, I can't compete with your video games. But I *need* your attention." I would say stuff like, "Let's have fun. Let's do this so we all have fun. If I'm not having fun, you certainly aren't gonna have any fun."

My second year there, they assigned me AP chemistry, two regular chemistry classes, and a physical science class, which was OK. But my third year at Sullivan, they gave me two seventh-grade classes, and the seventh-grade curriculum was human anatomy. So I just adapted my medical school textbooks to the task. I told parents, "What I'm doing is teaching your kids what I learned in medical school. We're using my textbooks. Even though they have a little textbook for their grade level, I'm teaching them something else." I was teaching my kids hormonal feedback loops, all about nerves and blood vessels. I didn't just do the basic things. I thought, "Why not? They can do it." There's no limit to what children can do, especially when they're interested and curious.

But because the seventh-grade classes were not labs, they also assigned me a study hall for the last period of the day, in the lunchroom. Because the seventh-grade students weren't at lab classes, my schedule was open enough that they could give me this kind of duty. I thought it was really messed up. This is what sent me over the edge at Sullivan—when they required me to teach middle-school kids *and* cover last-period study hall.

At the same time, one of my friends was completing her principal internship at Lane. She called me up one day—I'll never forget it. "Jennings, do you want to teach at Lane?" I told her not really. She didn't give up. "You could teach all chemistry classes. The chemistry teacher that just came in August said he wasn't coming back. Can you come in for an interview on Monday?" This was a Friday. I said sure.

I called my dad and asked him what he thought. "What's the big difference?" I wanted to know. He said, "Do you know how many teachers want to get into Lane?" He mentioned that one of the chemistry teachers at Kenwood was on the transfer list at that time and he never could get in. He told me it would be a great thing for me but reminded me that I was happy at Sullivan. "You created a niche for yourself, so it's really up to you." I did love the community at Sullivan, but I thought, "I can't do another year of last-period study hall in the lunchroom." I knew they would do it to me again.

That was enough of a reason. I decided to go to Lane. I gave the principal at Sullivan my transfer form, which he had to sign because it was after the deadline. He asked me why I was going, and I started making up all these different excuses. He said, "I'm not gonna stop you from a good opportunity."

Chapter 7

Growing

Right before I started teaching at Lane, I earned my MA in Inner City Studies Education at Northeastern Illinois University's Center for Inner City Studies on Thirty-Ninth Street. My experience at the Center for Inner City Studies reoriented me and reset my thinking. It informed my teaching, leadership, and fight for social justice. And it prepared me to be ready to fight in the years ahead.

When I was younger, before graduate school, I'd read *The Autobiography of Malcolm X* and all of Frantz Fanon. I read Fanon in English, and then I read it in French to make sure I understood it, to make sure I didn't miss anything in the translation. But I hadn't read any Chancellor Williams. I hadn't read John Henrik Clarke. I hadn't read Harold Cruse's *The Crisis of the Negro Intellectual*, which I really liked. I hadn't read any of these thinkers! When I got to Northeastern, these books were all on the reading lists, and I just *devoured* them. I would not only read the assigned readings, but I would also read them over and over again and take lots of notes in the margins. I'd annotate the *hell* out of my stuff. It was all new to me.

Taking classes with the guys (and most of them were guys) at the Center for Inner City Studies shaped me—Professor Anderson Thompson, Professor Robert Starks, Professor Conrad Worrill, and, of course, Professor Jacob Carruthers. Jacob Carruthers was wonderful. He reminded me of my grandfather. He was fun and smart as hell, and would make you defend an argument, which I appreciated. The other students, these dudes (and it was mostly dudes), would just start talking off the top of their heads. I would always question them, not in a challenging manner, but to say, "Where in the text is that? Can you show me where that is in the text? Maybe I read something else, because I'm not interpreting it the same way." I would explain, "If you look on page 397, paragraph 2, line 6, it says, 'blah blah blah blah,' and that completely contradicts what you just said." It was so intellectually stimulating. The recent debates about reparations are not new for me. My professors at Northeastern were talking about reparations in the 1980s and demanding reparations sooner, not later.

I was reading all this great nonfiction about Black history. Reading brilliant Black scholars whose work I hadn't read before and being in these conversations at the Center for Inner City Studies put me back on the road toward social justice again after having been off since the '60s. I loved Robin D. G. Kelley's work. I got to meet him later, and he's pretty damn cool too. Of everything I've read, my favorite is still John Henrik Clarke. He wrote with such clarity and dignity. He made things *right* for me. I never got the chance to meet him, but I did talk to him on the phone once. Dr. Anderson Thompson at the Center for Inner City Studies gave me his number, saying, "If you like him so much, you should call him and talk to him." We had a lovely chat. He told me, "I'm gonna write one more book, but if I write that book, they gon' sho' nuff kill me." Then he said it was his book about "the mulatto." I said, "Oooohhh, yes. Get 'em, get 'em, do it."

§

When I started teaching at Lane Tech High School in 1991, George Bush—the father—was president of the United States, Richie Daley—the son—was mayor of Chicago, and Jackie Vaughn—the esteemed first Black woman to lead the CTU—was still president of the CTU. As long as I worked there, Lane always required a test for students to get in—even before the growth of so many other selective enrollment schools when Daley was mayor. It was among the most competitive high schools in CPS, and with nearly four thousand students, it was the city's largest public school. Located on a huge campus in Roscoe Village on Chicago's North Side, Lane was founded in 1908 as a technical school and later became a college preparatory school. There were always some kind of prerequisites for admissions. Girls were not even admitted as students until 1971![1] Historically, it was overwhelmingly white. By the time I started teaching at Lane in the early 1990s, white students were still the largest group, but there was also a significant and growing Latinx student population and smaller populations of Asian American and Black students too.

At Lane, we didn't have just one science department because the building was so big. We had a biology department, a physics department, a chemistry department, and an earth science department. When I started at Lane, we had nine chemistry teachers! Years later, Lane is still *the* largest school in the district, with more than 4,500 students and more than 250 staff members.[2]

The building looks like a junior college because it was originally *supposed* to be a high school *and* a junior college. Way back in the day, junior colleges—which originated in Illinois around the turn of the twentieth century—were part of the Chicago Public School system. Early promoters of junior colleges thought the first two years of college should be for general education. Students could complete these years at high schools before moving on to more specialized programs of study.[3] I think it would make a lot of sense to offer junior college courses back in high school again; with dual credit and dual enrollment, kids could earn some City College credits while they're still in high school. And if City Colleges was in the CPS system again, it would be that much easier for students.

I was at Lane from 1991 until 2006, the majority of my time teaching. And for me, Lane was the most racist, sexist place I'd ever worked. I was always really aware of tensions there—I hadn't felt that way since I left Dartmouth. Around the time I started at Lane, only about 18 percent of the students were Black. The proportion of teachers of color was also small—only about one-third, compared to 56 percent citywide. In fact, the number of Black teachers and Black students declined at Lane during my time there. This was a pattern that Black teachers experienced across the district. When I started teaching in the 1980s, Black teachers outnumbered white teachers in CPS. By the time I left the classroom in 2010, less than 30 percent of teachers were Black.[4] Many of my coworkers at Lane were by and large pretty racist, although they would pretend they weren't: "I treat everybody the same." Well, yes, because then it's easier for you.

I was underwhelmed by Lane, and by the students at Lane, too. Everyone told me, "Oh, you're going to *love* the kids at Lane." No. However, compared to the kids at Sullivan, the kids at Lane *did* have an inherent silliness—Lane kids were funny as hell. They loved to giggle—they just loved it. And it was the same way at King, where I ended my teaching career—my students cracked me up on the regular there too.

When I met John, my husband, he had been teaching at Lane since 1971—the year the school went coed. Twenty years later, when I started teaching at Lane, he was still one of the few Black teachers there. The Black teachers kind of looked out for each other because we still felt ostracized and marginalized by other faculty and by leadership. But when I first arrived, I didn't get along well with John. I did get along really well with John's wife, Maxine McBryde, an English teacher at Lane. Maxine and I became friends. We remained tight until she passed away from cancer in 1994. I was devastated. But John and I still didn't really click; he was a good guy, but we both had confrontational streaks. And early on, I got his name wrong—I called him Coach McBryde because I assumed he and Maxine had the same last name. He did not like that much at all.

Like me, John was born and raised in Chicago and had come up through CPS, and a few of the kids he'd gone to school with also ended up becoming teachers—including his good friend Lauren Parker, who taught English at Lane. John was born in Bronzeville—53 West Thirty-Sixth Street—until his family was forced out as part of Mayor Richard J. Daley's urban renewal plan. They moved to 2350 South State Street in the Harold Ickes homes—public housing projects on the Near South Side, the Low End. John's mom raised him and his two sisters and two brothers. John was the baby and he loved his mama. He attended Raymond Elementary in Bronzeville and Haines Elementary in Chinatown before they redrew attendance lines to put most of the kids from the projects at Daniel

Hale Williams Elementary near the Dearborn Homes. Back then at Williams, they had all the kids from the projects plus some Italian kids from Twenty-Sixth Street and some Chinese kids from the Chinatown area. John always talks about what a good school Williams was and how great his teachers were. He graduated from Dunbar High School in Bronzeville when Neil F. Simeon—the legendary Black educator, vocational education innovator, and eventually one of the highest-ranking Black officials in CPS—was an administrator at the school. John was popular in high school; he played football, was all-city in swimming, ran track. And he was smart—always had good grades.

John's sister, Clara, was also a teacher. She had gone to CTC, but John graduated from Millikin University. Millikin was a small private college in Decatur, Illinois. John got a scholarship to play football there. But it was a difficult and alienating environment. John was one of just a handful of Black students at the almost all-white school in a very white part of central Illinois. When he graduated, he taught and coached cross-country and track in Decatur before coming back to Chicago and teaching physical education in CPS. He was thrilled when he was assigned to teach at his alma mater, Dunbar, and equally deflated when the board of education reassigned him to an elementary school on the North Side. In those days, the board was allegedly implementing faculty desegregation. This meant that after years of seemingly only being able to teach at Black schools, new Black teachers were now being assigned to schools with few Black teachers and few Black students, often far away from where they lived. John taught physical education briefly at an elementary school on the North Side, then briefly at Taft High School on the northwest side, before going to Lane in 1971, where he would spend the rest of his career teaching physical education.

The students at Lane loved John and Maxine because they were amazing teachers. John coached basketball and track—most of the kids just called him Coach. The kids were devoted to him. He always fought hard and advocated for them, and I liked that about him. He always had two managers for his teams, students who doted on him as he doted on them. He called them his little daughters. And they played a role in putting us together—at least this is how John would tell the story!

John and Maxine had gone to prom together every year at Lane to see off his graduating students. His managers, and some of his players, were encouraging him to take me to his first prom after Maxine passed, without my knowledge. John and I actually taught a lot of the same students. Later on, he told me that his students liked me because I was a good teacher and because I made chemistry fun. They got on him to take me to prom: "Coach, are you gonna take Miss Jennings?" In the meantime, these same students were encouraging me to go with him. They were telling him to ask me. And then they told him—when he was trying to back out—that I'd taken the day off of school to buy a dress to go with him. We finally got together, after these kids had been running games on us, and made a plan to go to the prom together. John asked me what color my dress was so that he could coordinate what he was wearing. He assured me that he would not pick me up in his van, which he used for games and meets. For the prom, he would bring the town car.

It was a platonic date, but because we really enjoyed each other's company, it was an absolutely amazing first date. Over time, we saw other people. I dated a professional football player for a while. But John and I would hang out a couple times a month and see shows—it was fun and it was easy. John knew I loved opera and theater, and because of Maxine, he had season tickets to the Lyric, the Studebaker, and the Goodman. We dated for a while before it became serious, and that was OK too. By the time we got together, more kids knew about us than adults at the school.

We got married in Hawai'i in 2001, with a small group of friends and family attending. John and I share a love of traveling—we've been to Mexico, the Italian Riviera, London, other spots in Europe—and we also love tennis. We went to New York City for the US Open to see my favorite player, Roger Federer.

And my husband is fine! He has big brown eyes, a beautiful smile, and a cute dimple. So those kids at Lane who set John and me up were playing the long, long game. And we won—they invited us back to their twentieth high school reunion. John is an introvert, but he can be semisocial. And he stays by my side and supports me in everything I want to do.

§

After John and I got together, I got my second master's degree, an MFA from Columbia College Chicago—this time in film. I was growing in lots of different ways during those years at Lane. My love for movies goes way back—me and my dad loved going to see the show when I was a kid. As an adult, I used to host an Oscars party every year. I've always liked entertaining people. Each year, the party had a different theme. I love to cook for people; it nurtures the soul. For the party, I would cook dishes that matched the theme. I served champagne and had my guests fill out ballots to guess the winners for best actor, best director, best film, etc. I took my Oscars party very seriously. As a child, I had always dreamed of winning an Oscar. I had my Oscar speech written by the time I was eight because I just knew I was gonna get one. And quite frankly, being CTU president was the closest thing to being an Oscar-winning actress. You're always out there, always out front. It's crazy, but you don't have to deal with the real craziness of Hollywood.

My appreciation for films led me back to school. I started in narrative film but switched to documentary film because I hated working with actors. I have no patience for grown people who are too needy. For my thesis, I had originally planned to do a film called *The Tale of Two Reunions*, comparing my twenty-fifth reunions from Mount Holyoke and from Dartmouth. The two reunions were so different in the way they sent out stuff for you to send back to participate in things. Mount Holyoke's said, "Tell us how you've changed in twenty-five years. Have you dyed your hair? Are your children grown yet?" It was basically encouraging alums to write an essay. Whereas Dartmouth's was, "Sign up for the 10K run. Sign up for the golf tournament. Sign up for the tennis tournament." And all I could think was, These old motherfuckers are going to come through here, and I'm gonna be standing at the end of the race line watching somebody pass out. And then I'm gonna fall out laughing. These Dartmouth guys were a mess. They were still competitive after all these years. Why couldn't we just get drunk in a tent and hang out and have a good time like we used to? Why did we have to compete with one another? That being said, at the time I also thought, "If I sign up for the tennis tournament, I'll whip all y'all's asses." So, for my documentary film thesis, I thought that it would be fun to look at these two reunions and how different they were going to be. But the timing of the reunions didn't work for my schedule.

Ultimately, I made a film for my thesis called *Search for Luciana*. It started as a conversation that I had with my cousin Tootsie about her father, my Uncle Bob. He had served in Italy during

World War II. I knew that because one day I was mad at his wife—my aunt Nanno, my mother's oldest sister—and, under my breath, I said, "*Pazza*!" And he looked at me and he said, "Ooh. *Parli Italiano*?" And I said, "*Si. Si, parlo Italiano*." I had picked up Italian during my time at Mount Holyoke on the Italian floor and to support my love of opera. So my uncle says, "OK. Maybe that's how we need to communicate from now on." And I said, "Sure, Uncle Bob, we can do that. But *pazza* means 'crazy,' you know. And your wife is."

So one day I was talking to my cousin Tootsie about something I had never heard before, that her father, Uncle Bob, initially wanted to name her Luciana. I said, "Really?" And she said yeah. When Uncle Bob was in Italy with the military, the Italian women loved to hang out with Black soldiers from the United States. And some of those soldiers left girlfriends and kids behind. Tootsie and I thought that maybe Uncle Bob had a girlfriend or a child back in Italy too. Maybe named Luciana. We decided we were going to find this Luciana. By the time I was working on the documentary, Uncle Bob was dead, so we couldn't ask him any direct questions. But we got his military service records and followed his company throughout Italy. We followed in his footsteps. That was my thesis film.

I was in Italy for two weeks around 2000 to shoot the film. John came with me and we traveled all over the Po River valley, north of Tuscany. It was wonderful. I love Italy. The footage from Italy is only part of my film. A lot of the footage that I used in the documentary came from the National Archives. With that film, I earned my MFA in 2002.

The board of education didn't want to give me a sabbatical to earn this second master's. When I asked why not, they told me, "Well, because the degree is not in education, and how do we know you won't go to Hollywood after you finish an MFA?" I said, "Because I'm not interested in Hollywood. And Hollywood wouldn't be interested in me. This is documentary that I'm interested in, and I'm too fat for Hollywood. You go to Hollywood; they don't pay any attention to you unless you're a size two! And that's never going to happen."

I ended up just resigning from my teaching position and then I re-upped. Luckily, I didn't lose any of my seniority, which was a good thing. And my principal at Lane promised me that I could come back. That was important. And I did go back to teaching at Lane for another few years, until 2006, when I moved to Martin Luther King Jr. College Preparatory High School.

§

I made the decision to move to King in part because I had gotten tired of my commute to Lane. I was excited for a shorter commute because I knew it would reduce my stress. At the worst of times, in the middle of the deep snow in winter, my commute to King from where I was living in Hyde Park was fifteen minutes. My commute to Lane, on the other hand, was usually an hour and a half. I ultimately moved out of Hyde Park because I couldn't afford to live in the neighborhood anymore, but John and I had been looking for a new place. I wanted to be in North Kenwood or Oakland because I wanted to be close to work. We found our current place—six blocks from King—and moved in around 2007. On top of everything else, I knew I couldn't continue working with the principal at Lane. So I expected the move to King would be a good change.

Like Lane, when I arrived at King—on the South Side, down the street from my home and near my native Hyde Park—they had to adjust to me. King had under nine hundred students at the time, much smaller than the four thousand plus students at Lane. King had been through a lot of changes, which made it feel a little crazy to me as a new teacher at the school. In the early 2000s, King had transitioned from a neighborhood high school to a selective enrollment school—where students had to test in and have high grades to attend. King was the first school I taught at that had a majority Black teaching staff. When I got there, there had been a *lot* of turnover in the school's administration. One of the principals came from a grammar school. And no matter how good the grammar school principal is, if they have no high school experience, I think it's usually a mistake for them to take that role at a high school. For one thing, high school teachers are more raucous than elementary school teachers. Generally, elementary school teachers are more compliant. You can get them to do just about anything because they overwork them to death. I don't know how anybody teaches elementary school—I take my hat off. Truly. As a high school teacher, I had periodic breaks, multiple prep periods where I wasn't in front of kids.

I taught at King from the 2006–2007 school year until 2010, when I was elected CTU president. My last few years of teaching at King were the absolute best. Why? Because I had common planning time with the other woman who taught chemistry, Shareda Newbern. We tweaked our curriculum daily. *Daily*! We could talk to each other about what worked and what didn't work. We both had first- and second-period classes. We were off for division, and we were off for the third period. And we spent that whole time, every single day, talking to each other. "Did that work for you?" we would ask each other. "Because that didn't work for me." Shareda and I had completely different views about how to teach chemistry. She was much more project-based, which I call coloring. I would tell her, "Girl, I can't do the coloring. It's too much." She had come from middle school, so she was used to dealing with younger kids. I'm more lab-based because I had also worked in industry in the summers. I had worked at Dow chemical company and at Searle pharmaceutical company. That's what I would do in the summers to keep my hands wet: analytical chemistry. That's the kind of stuff you don't retain and really lose if you don't use it.

Shareda and I were able to use our talents to work together to create a really good program at King. I got to understand the coloring projects better and I started utilizing techniques that were similar—if not quite hers exactly—and I dragged her ass into the lab.

Even when my kids were cracking me up, I could never forget that I was working in the most dangerous room in the building—the chemistry lab. I think Shareda was afraid of the lab and afraid she didn't have enough control over her kids. Her students always seemed to be a lot wilder than mine. She was younger too—I'm an old-ass woman. At first, the kids treated me funny because they thought I was new to teaching because I was new to King. So they tried to test me. As I started out, I wouldn't answer their questions—I would *ask* them questions . . . to get them to come to an answer. You know, teachers do have a way of doing that!

At first, the students complained about me. They went to their biology teacher, a young Black woman. At the first teachers' meeting, she came up to me and said, "The kids are telling me you don't answer their questions." And I looked at her and I said, "Does that make sense to you?" And she said, "Well, no." I said, "OK. How long have you been teaching?" She said, "Five years." I said, "I've been at this, *mmm*, eighteen or twenty . . . I'm National Board Certified . . . I think I kind of *know* what I'm doing." I paused, then asked, "Did you see what just happened here?" I said, "Let's talk about what happened here. You asked me a question. I didn't answer it. I asked *you* a question, to get you to the right answer." It's the Socratic method! It's been going on for *thousands* of years—training scholars, training physicians, lawyers, and whatnot. And then I gave her my "And what do you think about that?" look.

Over time, they've taken more and more autonomy away from teachers and really limited our ability to teach and to be responsive to our students' individual needs. Standardized testing, competition with charter schools, and the policies advanced by the 2001 No Child Left Behind Act and 2009 Race to the Top initiative have hurt public school teachers and students. Of course, my situation was a little different because most principals didn't know anything about chemistry. They might walk into my room—I could be doing anything—and they wouldn't understand. For the majority of my career, I taught in selective enrollment schools. I always had great kids—at Sullivan too—but at Lane and King, they were students who'd had to test into the schools, so my students' test scores were going to be high. My teaching settings were never difficult; I had glorious teaching experiences. But I also knew that many people were having much more stressful times as teachers. Magnet schools and selective enrollment schools—where I did the majority of my teaching—started as ways to integrate schools, a good idea. But that's not how it played out. If CPS can fuck it up, they will. Such is Murphy's law.

Still, I loved teaching. And I miss it so much. I miss that *spark* in a kid's face when they finally get it, because chemistry is so damn hard. I made it my goal to make chemistry accessible to kids. I didn't want to make it like, "I've got some secret information and you're going to have to figure it out." I hated teachers who approached chemistry and physics like that, and I happened to like both subjects. I'd been lucky enough to have a math teacher when I was in high school, Mrs. Lavington, who changed my entire life. She was so memorable and so formative to my education and to my own approach to teaching, I would call her first on Mother's Day. A few years ago, my husband, John, and I went to see her out in South Dakota. As a teacher, she was patient and did not assume we knew anything. And I remembered that when, years later, I was teaching chemistry.

In September, at the beginning of school, I would say, "You know *all* the chemistry I'm going to teach you. You just don't *know* you know it." And the students would say, "*What?*" The kids would look at me like I was from Mars. And I'd look at them and say, "Yes, you do! You know *all* the chemistry I'm going to teach you. You just don't *know* you know it. I'm going to pull it out of you." Then they'd all look at each other like, "This woman is *nuts*." On the first day of chemistry class, I would always do a demonstration, something to surprise them, like lighting some magnesium on fire.

Fire always brings people to the table; it glows and it is pretty. I'd define the differences between a chemical and a physical change by asking, "Which one is this?" And then I'd set some magnesium on fire, and those kids would look at me like I was crazy. I'd say, "A physical change is like a state of matter, like water goes from liquid to ice to water vapor, but it can always go back. But a chemical change you can't put back. Once you change, it's not a change in *state* of matter, it's a *change* of matter." All the kids know what matter is, because they've been taught that over the years. And so when I would ask them what matter was, they would tell me, and I said, "See? You already *know* what chemistry is. Chemistry is the study of *matter*." And they would go, "Ohhh. Yeah?" And I would go, "See? I *told* you!" And I said, "So, what do you think happened? Describe what happened. Matter of fact, write it down, so you'll get used to observing and then drawing conclusions from your observations."

I would tell them, "This is a *life skill*, honey. This is not just chemistry. You're supposed to be able to look at things and not just see what they are on the surface but note what you see *underneath*. If you understand this, you will never have any trouble at jobs or with politics. You'll be able to figure all this stuff out. You'll be able to hear somebody tell you one thing and you can see they're doing something else." I would always tell my students, "I'm not going to just teach you chemistry. I'm going to teach you *life*. Because you're going to need that." I thought that this was a better way to approach chemistry, instead of telling them, "This is the hardest class you're ever going to take in your life." Which happens to be pretty true, I think, except for physics. But it's not a useful way to approach teaching.

As a high school teacher, I saw kids change over the years. Over time, I'd say that my students actually seemed to know more, but they had less confidence. I also noticed that my kids were more and more frightened of being *wrong*, of making mistakes. And I used to tell my students all the time, "That's the only way you can *learn*. You can't learn if everything is steam-shoveled out of your way." And because so many people have difficult experiences in chemistry classes in particular, I was committed to introducing the subject differently and positively. I taught them how to do *real* labs and keep a *real* lab book, like you would if you were working in a chemistry lab for real. Over time, some kids would come back from good colleges and tell me, "Remember that lab we did? About so-and-so or so-and-so?" I'd say, "Yes, I do." And they'd say, "We did that in first-semester chemistry at Marquette." And I'd say, "Really? That's good. Because you were ready for it, right?" And they would say, "Yes, I was!" So I thought that was cool. That's the kind of stuff I liked hearing. Kids would come back to visit and tell me they felt totally prepared for chemistry in college.

I want my students to know how proud I am of them and the work they're doing now. I have a couple of former students who are now CTU delegates. And when I look out and I see them, I'm so proud. That's my heart. That's important to me. I spent a lot of time thinking about how to encourage my students. It wasn't just how I did lesson planning or whatever. It's how I took them aside and said, "You know what? You're brilliant. You've got *all* of these talents."

Most people have bad experiences in chemistry classes because it's such an abstract discipline: I can't show you a proton, I can't show you the nucleus, I can't show you an atom. We have to pretend. One of the things that would annoy me the most is when other teachers used this solar system model to explain atoms. I didn't like that, because that's not what all atoms really look like—it depends on the atom! "Here's the deal," I would say. "You have to think about the Heisenberg uncertainty principle: Any instrument that measures the velocity of the particles of atoms would *change the position* of where they are, and any instrument that would measure the position would change the speed or the velocity at which atoms move. You can't do one without messing up the other!" That's why, just like religion, you have to take it on faith.

Chapter 8

My Faith

My favorite line in *Yentl* is when the rabbi says, “It’s by their questions that we choose our students, not only by their answers.” I loved this whole notion of study, study, study—you’re never done studying. And while people like to separate religion and science, I believe my faith in chemistry resonates with my religious faith. I understand the reasons for the separation—they are not alike—but you can use each to explore and expand the other.

I was early in my teaching career when I was coming into Judaism. Coming to teaching and coming to Judaism were related for me; I had resisted teaching because that’s what both my parents did, and I had resisted religion because I wasn’t finding what I needed in Christianity. The fact that these quests came to fruition around the same time was very helpful, and probably not coincidental.

When I was growing up, my parents encouraged curiosity until it got on their nerves. That happened whenever they had to explain complicated things they didn’t really want to get into—which was certainly a feature of our discussions about sex and religion. And the less their explanations made sense to me, the more I wanted to discuss the issues with an analytical eye. Why was sex a beautiful thing when you're married, I wanted to know, but not before? How did a piece of paper make that kind of difference? And I've *never* gotten Jesus. Even as a little kid, Jesus worried me. At a young age, I informed my mother that I liked Big God, but I didn't like Little God. If God is God, how can Jesus, who was a man, be God? And why would you pray to a man? "It's called faith," my mother would say.

When I was about twelve, I told my parents I was an atheist. At the time, I was more interested in science and science fiction and felt I had outgrown "mythology." In my opinion, you can't call yourself a Christian if you don't believe in Jesus Christ. And it was hard for me to ever understand the notion of a *man* being God, and then follow the requirement to worship this man. How do you make the choice to believe in someone who actually walked this earth? For me, this was a huge challenge—it was not logical, and it didn't feel right—and pressing the issue got me kicked out of confirmation class when I was a kid. Because I kept asking questions. Nobody could ever answer my questions or, more importantly, really address my need to understand. And since you can't call yourself a Christian if you don't believe in Christ, I left Christianity.

My mother wasn't having it at first. She said, "We're all going to go back to church!" "Why?" I asked. "Because we are a Christian family!" She was emphatic, and I was confused. We didn't go to church regularly, but this time I hung my head and said OK. We went to church the following Sunday. Keli, then just a toddler, wore a beautiful yellow dress with white dots and white patent leather shoes. She stood on the pew and peered at the adults in the row ahead of us. She asked in that sweet little-kid voice,

"Mama, is that God?" as she pointed to the pastor. I thought that was the funniest thing ever and remarked a bit snidely, "Oh yeah, we're a good Christian family. The baby thinks the preacher is God." My mother tried to swat me, but I ducked and continued giggling through the Agnus Dei.

We were Lutherans, and I always found church to be a chore. We went the following week, but that was that. Even my parents couldn't keep up with the rigors of weekly churchgoing. What's funny is that I knew they couldn't keep up with it. I got up that third Sunday, put my good clothes on, and looked around. My parents were still in their casual clothes. So I asked, "What time are we going to church?" "Oh," my mother responded offhandedly, "we're not going this week; we have some things to do." I started down the hallway, and when I got out of earshot, I howled in laughter. I knew it! I knew they couldn't keep it up!

I did not like church at all, and part of my disinterest came from the fact that our Lutheran church wasn't ritualistic enough. If my parents' church had been more entertaining and offered a bit more pizzazz, maybe I would have enjoyed it more. I always liked going to my grandmother's church—Bray Temple CME. Now, that was a fun one. When I was a little kid, Bray Temple was at 5333 South Indiana, just a little bit to the west of where we lived, but they moved to a new building in 1961 on Seventy-Third Street in the Grand Crossing neighborhood, further south from where we lived. It was entertaining! But even Bray wasn't as much fun as a good, solid, Baptist down-home kind of church. Our Lutheran church was like Catholicism without any showbiz. And I like a little bit of showbiz in my religion. Had I believed in Jesus, I probably would either have been Catholic or Greek Orthodox. I'd looked up Coptic churches, and they seemed to be interesting, with more pomp and circumstance too. This is part of what drew me to Judaism—there's a *whooole* lot of showbiz.

After leaving Christianity and declaring myself an atheist at twelve, it wasn't until I was a grown adult that I chose to become a Jew. The religion touched and moved me in ways nothing else had. I'd joined a more activist Lutheran church in Tulsa in the 1970s, but it still didn't give me what I needed—something spiritual. So I came to Judaism when I was in my late thirties. I think every woman either comes into her own around that time, or she collapses.

While I enjoy ritual and faith, I need opportunities to discuss, debate, and interpret, not just rules and regulations. For example, I love Shabbat morning services—they just felt very familiar and comfortable. There are practices in Judaism that are very similar to the call-and-response tradition in the Black church. There are many customs and practices straight out of Judaism that you can see analogies to in other faiths. We talk a lot in this country about our Judeo-Christian values, but I was always asking, where is the social justice, where is the "Love thy neighbor," and where is the "There shall be no needy"?

My conversion started in the late 1980s, but my first exposure to Judaism occurred when I was in high school. There were a lot of Jews in Hyde Park at that time, and I went to high school with a lot of Jews. It was interesting to me that some of them were very religious, and some of them were very secular—there didn't seem to be a middle ground. They were either very Orthodox and very traditional, or they were social justice Jews. The second thing that prompted my curiosity was the 1983 Barbra Streisand movie, *Yentl.* The movie presented Judaism as a religion of lifelong learning, which strongly appealed to me. As did a religion that supports people figuring it out on their own, as opposed to belief for the sake of belief. Because, you know, if you ask questions in the Christian church, you get told, "You have to take it on faith." For a kid with a good mind, that's not always enough.

I started to more seriously explore Judaism and consider converting in the late 1980s and early 1990s. A friend of mine invited me to Kol Nidre (the evening service for Yom Kippur) at Congregation Rodfei Zedek. When I went to the synagogue for the service, I saw a couple of my friends from high school. And I was so taken by the experience. It was ritualistic, it was beautiful. And it really spoke to me—it's all about atoning for your sins. Some of the sins people named were hilarious, like backbiting, you know, just all kinds of stuff. People shared a list of things that you should say: "I'm not gonna do it anymore." It might seem basic, but it was just so moving to me. I said, "This is it! This is where I want to be!" I was teaching at Sullivan at the time. I had Jewish friends from teaching, too, and I was already going to Seders and stuff. I thought, "Man, I might as well just go on and join the tribe!"

One of my old friends from high school, Jeffrey Blumenthal, belonged to the synagogue. I saw him that night at Kol Nidre and said, "Man, I want to be a Jew so bad." And he said, "Well, I'll introduce you to the rabbi." Because Jeffrey and his family were mucky mucks, what they call big machers in the shul. The fact that he was the one who brought me in was important. And now, I'm a macher.

That night at Kol Nidre, Jeffrey introduced me to the rabbi—Rabbi Gertel. Now, technically, the rabbi's supposed to discourage you three times from becoming a Jew. He never did! He just said, "Oh, you wanna be a Jew? OK." And he laid out what I would have to do. He sent me to classes at Spertus

College, a Chicago higher-education institution focused on Hebrew and Jewish culture, and I had to learn to read Hebrew. Learning Hebrew appealed to me, too, as someone who loved learning languages. I had to learn to read it and to pronounce the words, but I didn't really learn any hardcore grammar at Spertus.

As I was preparing to convert, I would also have meetings with Rabbi Gertel in his study, and we would talk about things. We had wonderful conversations, and eventually he said, "You know, I think you're ready." So I converted to Judaism.

§

When I did convert, my father loved it. He thought it was hilarious, you know? He'd always been fascinated with Judaism—he loved klezmer music, Jewish folk music. My mother, on the other hand, was horrified for my eternal soul. My sister was OK. You know, even though she's now a really serious born-again Christian, she was OK with it. When I first converted, my sister was in her late twenties. My mom—the least religious member of our family!—was the most worried. I thought this was hilarious.

After converting, I did step away from Judaism, on and off. But I kept coming back to Judaism on a regular basis because I felt I *needed* it. When I converted, I was staring down forty and I was looking for something spiritual. I needed something that was prescribed and circumscribed. Later, when I started working with the CTU and had such a highly visible role, I needed that comfort even more intensely because I felt attacked so much. Having religion at that time was really important for me. I needed to circle the wagons!

Some things made me question my faith, namely about Israel and the whole Palestinian piece. I had some real conflicts about that. Unlike most Jews, I don't have a familial or cultural connection to Israel. So I regard the people of Israel differently than I regard the government. The people? Yes. The government? Not so much. I take solace in a prayer that always brings me peace: "My God, keep my tongue from evil, my lips from lies . . ."

In the prayer book, after that comes the prayer for Israel, which I never say. I have looked at Judaism as my religion, as opposed to the political side of Judaism, which manifests itself in the state of Israel. I kind of understand this on one level, but on the other level, I don't. I'm not a Zionist. There have been stretches where I didn't go to shul for months because I was struggling to navigate between my faith and the actions of the Israeli government. And it made me question my faith on *several* levels, until I realized there's a difference between politics and faith. I don't live over there, and I've never been. But I know that there's an apartheid system in Israel and I don't like that. As a *Black* Jew, I feel like I understand that part. Because being Black, you feel oppression all the time.

I'm also more of a quasi-religious Jew because I don't keep kosher. If I had children, I would, but I don't. It's hard. You've gotta be really committed to that. But I enjoy being a Jew—it gives me comfort. I think that's what religion is *supposed* to do for you. But I see that for so many people who practice, religion doesn't give them comfort, it oppresses them. And I think it's important not to be oppressed—period—by whatever it is you do. Throw off those shackles.

§

A decade after I converted, I decided to make a deeper commitment to my faith by becoming a Bat Mitzvah. I knew that the Bat Mitzvah itself would take more commitment, but I thought it would make me feel whole, like a completion process. And I really enjoyed it. My rabbi picked the parasha—the Torah portion for my Bat Mitzvah—for me. He selected Shelach Lecha, from Numbers and Joshua 2, verses 1 through 24. I thought it was a good parasha for me because it challenged the idea of winners and losers. It was sort of like, "You can't fight Rahm Emanuel and city hall alone and win." So we took everybody out and put twenty thousand people in the street! I found this narrative very, very enlightening, and the parasha was even more meaningful because my rabbi picked it for me. He didn't tell me directly why he picked that parasha, but it was clear to me.

I also discovered that Bat Mitzvahs for adult converts are a big thing. Completing the process requires a lot of discipline, practice, and work. It was 2013, and we were just a few months past our historic strike and were now implementing our first CTU contract as union leadership. And Robert Bloch, the CTU general counsel and my dear friend, is a Bat and Bar Mitzvah tutor at his shul, so he said, "I'll help you!" He was very serious. We would be in caucus, and he'd pull out his iPhone and say, "OK! C'mon, let's go, let's hear it. Do your parasha right now." So I would start solemnly reciting those several bars in Hebrew.

After lots of studying and preparation, I had my Bat Mitzvah on June 1, 2013. And after reading my parasha, I gave my D'var Torah, which translates as "words of Torah." But it's really an opportunity to give your interpretation of your parasha and teach the congregation something important from the Torah portion and share your ideas and beliefs with the community. This is what I said for my D'var Torah:

First of all, thank you, Rabbi Gertel, for finding this amazing parasha for me. I would not be here if you hadn't converted me twenty years ago, and before you retire, you needed to do this one last thing. Cantor Rachel Rosenberg, who has the voice of an angel and the patience of Job, to Reb Allan Olbur, who made a Bat Mitzvah package for me, including a wonderful recording, and to my tutor, Robert Bloch—the scariest of all. Thank you all for leading me on a path of internal reflection that is ultimately at the heart of Judaism. Thank you, Congregation Rodfei Zedek, for being the welcoming, intellectually stimulating spiritual home I need. Thanks to my family and friends who have come from both coasts and in between to share this amazing day with me. And thank you to my husband, John, who really is Job.

When I first read the Torah portion, there were three issues that struck me. God told the people of Israel, "I have given you this land. Take forty days, go check it out, and prepare yourselves to take possession." Good start. Twelve men went forward; ten came back and said, "We can't do it. Their cities are too well fortified, and we seem to be grasshoppers." Notice they didn't say, "Those guys thought we were grasshoppers." They said, "We appeared to be grasshoppers to ourselves." Only Caleb, who told folks to stop moaning and groaning, and Joshua, who said, "If this is what God says we can do, *sí se puede*!" So what did the Israelites say? "Aw no—let's just go back to Egypt. Even though we were slaves, it was better there than to come here and die." When God threatens to smite the entire population, Moses makes a plea to spare the people. Not because they are deserving, but because the Egyptians, Amelekites, et al. would think God was weak and couldn't bring the people to the Promised Land. God relents a bit, spares Caleb and Joshua, but tells everyone else, "*You* can't go, and *you* can't go, and your children will suffer for forty years!" Wow, that's harsh for just moaning. And, of course, some folks didn't believe the Lord and ran toward Canaan, only to be mowed down.

Let's unpack these issues and place them in context for today. What are some of the challenges the Israelites faced? Why were they willing to go back into slavery and why is God so demanding of loyalty? While the Israelites faced the challenge of terrain—mountains, the Sea of Reeds—we face a society in which some dominate and others are dominated. What does domination do to people? It tears the very fabric of self-esteem apart at the seams. Those who dominate are those who feel entitled to rearrange the world as they see fit. If you were to ask, "Who are the winners and losers?" the dominators always win. Why? Because who made the rules to the game? They did. They always win because whenever it looks as if they might lose, they simply change the rules. But what happens to the dominated? They often accept the confines of the world oriented by the dominators.

It is easy to believe one does not deserve decent wages, housing, and education, or a life filled with joy, especially if you get a consistent message that you are not worthy. So what are the stories that the winners tell the losers to keep them playing the game? The answer to that question is the key to unlocking real freedom from domination. Those three questions should always guide your decision-making process, and I owe a debt of gratitude to another Black Jew, Lani Guinier, for her elegant solution to a very complex set of problems.

Why would the Israelites choose to go back into slavery? Unfortunately, the shackles of servitude can encircle the mind long after the physical bonds have been broken. We are always more afraid of the unknown than the evil we know. Because God gave us free will, our imaginations tend to run wild. According to the great prophet of *Dune*, Frank Herbert, "Fear is the mind-killer." How does one, then, become a citizen of a new world order rather than a slave? Danielle S. Allen, author of *Talking to Strangers: Anxieties of Citizenship since Brown v. Board of Education*, says that "habits of citizenship begin with how citizens imagine their political world."

In the Torah portion, the ten spies saw themselves as grasshoppers—they clearly were not, but they felt defeated before they even started. But they had no way of feeling confident to talk to the strangers, let alone defeat them militarily. When they returned, the people of Israel internalized that defeat and let it be known. Slaves to domination, they were unable to allow themselves to take what God had given them. So not only did they not have confidence, they were punished again: God tells them, "I sent you out for forty days to reconnoiter the land and you will wander forty years." Your carcasses will drop. Wow. The ability to see oneself as unsuccessful can have so many unintended consequences, but the notion that one can be punished over and over again rears its ugly head even today. This is evinced in the notion that if one is convicted of a felony drug crime, even after serving time, it is impossible to obtain federal financial aid to go to school, food stamps, federally subsidized housing. And in some states, complete disenfranchisement. The punishment never ceases.

The Haftorah, which comes from the word meaning "completion," tells a very different story some forty years later. These two spies are coming to scout out the land before they wipe out all the inhabitants. One of the most beautiful lines lyrically roughly translates to, "Tell your mama, your daddy, and your whole generation to get inside your house. Anyone on the outside??? Oh well." It took forty years, but the winners and losers are very different.

My fear is that the battles we fought forty years ago are far from over. Now, the winners are a very small subset and the losers don't often realize they're losers. They accept the stories the winners tell that keep them playing the game. But the real losers in this battle of dominators and dominated are all of us. Those of us who think we've made it, those of us who think material success is the only goal that proves our worth, and those of us who know that there is so much more to life. Those of us who will be on the right side of history are those who listen to the teachings of Torah, who understand the meaning of *tsedek*, righteousness, and seek to practice. We all have choices. Let's choose to live lives of tsedek. Shabbat Shalom!

People clapped after I spoke. They aren't supposed to, but they did. I've been told that it's a very Black and bluesy interpretation and I agree with that. Being a Black Jew is interesting. It dawned on me that that's why Black people love the Lord so, because they can find their lives in it, *allll* the way through. And the whole notion of the Jews being slaves is very real. The three questions that I mention in my D'var Torah—Who are the winners and losers? Who makes the rules to the game? What stories do the winners tell the losers that keep them playing the game?—came from Lani Guinier, a Black Jew who has been my heroine for thirty years! I was reading her work in the early 1990s, when Bill Clinton tried to have her serve as Assistant Attorney General for Civil Rights at the Department of Justice, but later withdrew her nomination after Republicans attacked her work on voting rights and affirmative action and pejoratively called her the "quota queen."[1] I use these questions in almost every speech I make. I talk about it all the time because I think it's something that people need to think about.

I have had a relatively multicultural, multiracial experience of Judaism, including in my experience preparing for my Bat Mitzvah. One of my friends was Latina. Matter of fact, she gave me a parasha at her Bat Mitzvah. My Hagbah—that's the guy that carries the Torah around—was a guy named Kenzo Shibata. We call him a Jew-panese: his mother's Jewish, his father's Japanese. He's also really involved in the union. Randi Weingarten, president of the AFT, flew in for my Bat Mitzvah. I was asked to teach a class for "Jews by choice" at the shul. I considered it. Not this year, for sure, but maybe next year.

You know, very few people *know* I'm a Jew. And they'll notice it because a lot of times I wear a Magen David—Star of David. And I have a big ignorant one. I got it in Puerto Vallarta, of all places. My cousin convinced me—they were buying silver—and they convinced me to buy it. So when I was teaching and the kids would see my Star of David, they would ask me, was I a GD? And

I would laugh. "A *Gangster Disciple*, *really*? Look at me! A GD?" I said, "Do you even know why the Star of David, the Magen David, is a GD symbol? Because when they first started being GDs, they were meeting in the basement of an old Jewish community center and there were Stars of David all over, and they chose that as their symbol."

I have lots of Magen Davids and lots of beautiful Judaica in my home. I have several menorahs. I have my Sabbath candles. I have a tzedakah box, which is what you put money in for the poor . . . your charity box. Lots of tallits. I have five. I went into the store and lost my mind. My favorite piece of Judaica is my Seder plate that Bloch bought for me in Morocco.

I'm a big macher now at the shul. I used to come *every* Saturday. But since I've been working and since I got sick—not so much. Sometimes I just don't feel like getting up on Saturdays. I light my candles Friday night, watch them burn, and then go to bed. But eighteen minutes before sundown!

I like Shabbat Saturday services better than Friday night services. Friday night services are a little too casual for my taste. Give me the Torah, marching around, all that kind of stuff. I like the ceremony and the ritual. Dance around with the Torah and then bring out the Haftorah, which is the rest of the Bible that includes the prophets. The Torah tropes are in a major key and the Haftorah tropes are in a minor key. I personally like the Haftorah better. I think they're just more beautiful. And, to me, easier to learn. I haven't learned Torah tropes yet. With Torah, there are no vowels and there are no diacritical marks. So you have to really know it to read that.

Part of why Conservative Judaism fits me is because you get your Halacha laws (Jewish law, or practices, customs, traditions) and you get your pomp and circumstance, but you also get to learn a new language, which I liked a lot. A lot of the people at my shul are old. Conservatism is a branch of Judaism that's dying out—as soon as the members die out, they die out. If you're going to live halachically, you might as well be Modern Orthodox. And if you're going to live more secularly, you might as well be Reform. But I like that midrange. My synagogue speaks to my values. The name of my synagogue is Rodfei Zedek: "pursuers of righteousness."

My experience with religion now is so separate from my childhood experience. I like this better. It suits me more. It's intellectually stimulating and spiritually stimulating. My sister is Christian and probably the most religious member of my family, but she's been very supportive. I give her props for that. And part of it is that we grew up believing in that whole notion of tolerance. What I appreciated most about what my parents provided for us was the space to learn what's right and wrong, true and false, with space for people who are different and people who have other challenges. We knew that they weren't any better, nor were they any worse than we were. I love that I grew up in this way; I grew up thinking people were inherently equal. How radical!

My faith continues to renew me. I feel stronger and no longer helpless in the wake of a frightening health scare. It's made difficult decisions easier, and it's made it easier for me to remove toxic people and situations from my purview. It's made it easier to pray for wisdom, peace, and patience. I still believe in God, and I still believe in redemption, and I still believe that God loves us all and that you have to find your way *to* him. And on some level, everybody does find their way to God or *a* God or to whatever they're calling God this week. They find their way.

Chapter 9

A Labor Awakening

The foundation of union work is classroom work. It's the *foundation*. In my opinion, if you aren't a good teacher, you'll never be a good unionist. You have to love your students. You really do. If you don't love them, then what are you there for? What's the purpose of your work?

Every year I fell in love with my students when they walked through the door. And at the start of every year, I always thought, "It's not going to be the same, it's not going to be the same! So-and-so and so-and-so from last year aren't here anymore!" But then the next group of kids would walk in, and I'd fall in love with them all over again. I always loved my kids. How could I not?

When you teach for a long time, you see your students change: the things they care about, what they're observing, the kinds of questions they ask—and students ask the funniest things. But I'll tell you one thing that they *alllll* ask me, the chemistry teacher: "Do you know how to make a bomb?" And I say, "Yes, I do, but I'm not gon' teach you how." They always asked me that.

Most years, I taught about 140 kids—I had at least twenty-six students in each class, and I taught five classes. When I first started teaching, I had four classes. Later, CPS changed the schedule, so we'd teach five classes with shorter times for each period. When I had four classes, I taught eighty-minute classes, with labs, twice a week. Then they decided to make every class fifty minutes because "that's the way they do it in the suburbs." We would hear that *all* the time. "That's the way they do it in the suburbs." But we weren't in the suburbs. How are they comparing apples and oranges? We also didn't have the resources suburban schools and teachers have. On top of everything else, the other teachers who had division room duties—like English and history teachers—would get mad at science teachers because, for a while, we taught four classes and ran labs with no homeroom and they taught five. Over time, I would get really angry with administrators about these policy and practice decisions that didn't make any sense pedagogically at the classroom level. I think this was how I started to decide that I also wanted to be an advocate.

One of the first things I did at Lane was become one of the teacher members of the Local School Council (LSC). LSCs were instituted in CPS in the late 1980s right after Mayor Harold Washington's death. They were created at the state level with the Chicago School Reform Act of 1988, after years of calls from parents and community organizations to decentralize power and decision-making in CPS schools. Operating like mini–school boards for each school in Chicago, they include the principal, parents, teachers, and community members, and they hire and evaluate principals and make some budget decisions. Only a few years later, the LSCs' powers were diminished by the Chicago School Reform Act of 1995, which also put CPS under mayoral control. I was on the LSC at Lane in the 1990s. But I only stayed on for one term—I ended up hating it. It was clear to me that the principal was influencing and controlling a group of parents on the LSC, and the teachers were always outvoted. Eventually, I came to feel that the principal abused his power and rewarded people loyal to him. I decided that it was not what I needed to be doing. Maybe instead, I needed to be more involved in the union. I saw the union as the only protection against unfairness.

There was an opening for an associate union delegate at Lane, and my husband encouraged me to run for it. He had also been an associate delegate. He told me I should do it, and I did. John is always my biggest supporter. I ran for the position and won, overwhelmingly beating the candidate that the school leadership had supported. It helped that I knew everybody at the school—I was popular! Because Lane was so big, we had multiple delegates and associate delegates.

Once I became a delegate, I started writing a little column; I called it "Brothers and Sisters of the Struggle." I later used a version of this as the title of the column I wrote for the *Chicago Union Teacher* when I was CTU president. In it, I would tell people what happened at the union meetings. People wouldn't usually go to the union meetings at Lane, but I didn't think it was fair to do what other people had done before me. In the past, when people would ask, "What happened at the union meeting? What happened at the LSC meeting?" they would be told, "You should havc bccn thcrc." I tricd to kccp pcoplc informcd through the column, drawing on my "journalism experience" once again. I put copies in everybody's mailboxes, and people got used to getting my updates. 'Ihey liked being informed. lt made them feel more involved in the union.

§

The CTU gained bargaining rights in the 1960s. But the CTU has been around in its current form since the 1930s and as the Chicago Teachers Federation since the 1890s. The CTU is Local 1 of the American Federation of Teachers (AFT) and has historically been an important player within the AFT. In the 1960s, when my parents first started teaching, the CTU was pretty tight with the Chicago Democratic machine and did not treat Black teachers well. At that time, the CTU leadership opposed desegregation for students and staff and supported practices that kept Black teachers in precarious full-time substitute positions and prevented them from becoming certified teachers. In the late 1960s, when I was protesting as a student at Kenwood, many of the Black teachers who supported us were also organizing for their rights, including greater inclusion within the union. And they were successful.[1]

By the 1970s, the United Progressive Caucus (UPC) was elected to power, with Jackie Vaughn as the first Black vice president of the CTU. The CTU had different caucuses in power over the years. The UPC was in power for almost three decades straight and went on strike multiple times. Jackie Vaughn was elected president of the CTU in 1984. She was the first African American and first woman to lead the CTU. Jackie was president when I started my teaching career at Sullivan in 1988. I thought she was amazing. Unfortunately, she died tragically of cancer at the age of fifty-eight in 1994.

Howard Heath was a Black math teacher at Lane, and he recruited me to serve as a delegate for the AFT convention. He also encouraged me to take on leadership roles in the union. John and Howard both really talked me into getting more involved in the union and serving as a delegate. Being a Black delegate at Lane was a big deal, since the school still had a predominantly white teaching force and overwhelmingly white delegates. After mayoral control of CPS went into effect in 1995—the year after Jackie Vaughn's death—members were mad about the way the UPC went along with the mayor and his administration. People were also mad about the way that the UPC negotiated the contract in 1998; many teachers felt they had given up too much at the bargaining table. An alternative caucus emerged to challenge the UPC: the ProActive Chicago Teachers (PACT) caucus. My friend Howard was with PACT and was elected to the executive board for the high schools in 1998 in an upset. In 2001, with Howard as her vice president, Debbie Lynch, a white elementary school teacher with PACT, ran against CTU president and UPC leader Tom Reece. PACT won the election, and Debbie Lynch and Howard Heath became president and vice president of the CTU.

I was a delegate then and was also serving on the executive board of the CTU. After a while, Debbie realized I had some insight. I also taught at Lane, the biggest high school in the city, which meant I had the ability to bring those teachers to the voting booth. So she put me on her advisory panel. Several people had asked me to be a part of their caucuses and to step out. But I didn't trust their politics or their vision for the union, so I didn't involve myself with those caucuses. With Debbie and Howard, it felt different. While I didn't agree with all of the PACT reforms, I appreciated the emphasis on teacher professionalism and the attempt to restore our bargaining rights.

But PACT's time in leadership was short-lived. People were mad about the 2003 contract under Debbie Lynch. The revamped "New UPC" ran its initial campaign against her based on how terrible the contract was. People would wave the contract in the air and boo every time Lynch came to the microphone. While high school staff overwhelmingly voted for the PACT caucus, PACT leadership lost their reelection bid in 2004. Elementary school staff and paraprofessionals voted for the "old guard," the New UPC, with Marilyn Stewart as president.

By this time, I was disillusioned with the union. I had served four tedious years on the executive board of the CTU, and fights in the CTU House of Delegates had gotten nastier while delegate attendance dropped. It was a rough few years, and I kept finding myself saying, "Oh God, I have to go to these meetings." I eventually stopped going—I found that the executive board meetings were just rehearsals for the house meetings. I thought it was a waste of my time.

When I transferred to King in the 2006–2007 school year, the delegate there asked me to help him because we had served on the executive board together. We ended up getting a second delegate at King because the faculty was large enough to qualify for additional representation. I ran and won. I was going to the house meetings, and I put out my regular memo to share what happened at the meetings, like I had done at Lane, but otherwise I was kind of checked out from union drama.

§

In 2008, Debby Pope called me up and said that Jesse Sharkey was involved in starting a new caucus. Jesse, a history teacher at Senn High School, was working with Jackson Potter and some others to start a new progressive caucus within the CTU. I met Jesse when I was on the advisory board for previous CTU president Debbie Lynch. Jesse and I had been pretty close in PACT. We both taught at North Side high schools. And what I liked about Jesse was that he was smart but not arrogant. He was a nice guy but he was also *brilliant*. I appreciated his ability to put a sharp point on an argument and to press an issue to a logical conclusion. He knew a lot about stuff I didn't know anything about. Like I didn't know anything about socialism, or lefty politics, or what any of that meant. People always called me a socialist, and I would ask Jesse, "Am I a socialist?" And Jesse would say, "You might be like the European socialists, like a democratic socialist." I didn't know about that, but I did learn a lot from Jesse.

In 2004, Jesse put up a massive resistance to the takeover of Senn by the military. The board of education wanted to put a naval academy into Senn as a pipeline for CPS students to enter the navy. With the ongoing US wars in Iraq and Afghanistan, there was a strong antiwar protest movement by teachers, parents, and community members who fought back against the plan. Jesse was a leader in that fight. Ultimately, the board of education did put the military program in the high school. But Jesse's willingness and ability to fight and his organizing skills made me want to do better work in organizing my building.

So when our mutual friend Debby Pope, who had also been active in PACT, told me Jesse was involved in starting a new caucus, I was intrigued. She asked whether I would come to a meeting. I agreed, so one hot and muggy April day in 2008, my husband John and I walked up three flights of creaky stairs to Casa Aztlan—an important center for Mexican arts, culture, and community at Eighteenth and Racine, in the Pilsen neighborhood on the Lower West Side.

We liked it. It wasn't a big group, but there were some familiar faces—the more radical members of PACT and a coterie of young, earnest-looking folks. They wanted to center the needs of students, parents, and community organizations working with young people. By the end of the meeting, we had homework assignments. They really caught me because it was a book club too, and I'm such a nerd. All I read is nonfiction anyway, so I was totally into it.

Reading and studying sharpened my analysis of these new school "reforms" and "school reformers" and the challenges facing public schools. We read Naomi Klein's *The Shock Doctrine: The Rise of Disaster Capitalism*, which is about how capitalism exploits catastrophes of nature and war to push privatization and profit, to the detriment of those most impacted by the disasters. It changed my life. During my preparation to teach, I had read Paulo Freire's *Pedagogy of the Oppressed.* Together with *Shock Doctrine*, I was able to connect the dots between the so-called school reformers and the Wall Street fat cats ushering in a new golden age of robber barons that was devastating our schools and communities. We read articles by Pauline Lipman, a professor at the University of Illinois Chicago, who studies the effects of school reform. She denounced the much-touted Renaissance 2010 plan—announced by Mayor Daley and CPS in 2004—as nothing more than a real estate plan concocted by the Civic Committee of the Commercial Club of Chicago, an elite group of corporate executives in the city with an outsized influence on public policy.

Renaissance 2010 outlined the opening of 100 new schools, mostly charter and contract schools, and the closure or "turnaround" of existing schools that they deemed to be failing. But they were opening these new charter and privately managed schools in mainly Black communities that were already experiencing declining enrollment. It created a terrible form of competition between schools for a shrinking number of students. In turnarounds, they get rid of everybody—not just the principals, teachers, and paraprofessionals, but the lunchroom ladies too. All staff members would be fired and then have to reapply for their jobs. It also included imposing new school models on existing schools, like the plan for a military academy at Senn. It was a vast expansion of privatization, "school choice," and market-based school reform in CPS. The ideas behind Renaissance 2010—privatization, charter school expansion, and "reconstitution" (the predecessor to turnaround)—started under Paul Vallas, the first CPS CEO that Mayor Richard M. Daley appointed when he took control of the schools in 1995.

Vallas held the role of CEO from 1995 to 2001. He increased the school system's reliance on standardized testing, used students' test scores to put schools on probation, stifled teachers' creativity, stripped teachers of their professional expertise by requiring back-to-basics scripted lesson plans, and implemented reconstitution, which, like turnaround, facilitated firing all school staff and then requiring them to reapply for their jobs. Assistant principals were also taken out of the union during this time. And Vallas more generally oversaw and ushered in the privatization of public education through the use of private consultants and private management firms and the opening of the first privately managed charter schools in the city.[2]

I saw Vallas go on to ruin the systems in Philadelphia and New Orleans through privatization and charter expansion before he finally got his educational comeuppance as superintendent of schools in Bridgeport, Connecticut. In June 2013, a Connecticut court ordered that Vallas "be removed from his office" because he had never taken graduate courses in education, didn't have the certification needed to be superintendent, and had not adequately completed an independent study program with already "reduced" course standards in an attempt to fulfill the requirement. The case was dismissed on appeal by the state supreme court, but only after Vallas had already stepped down as superintendent to run for lieutenant governor of Illinois.[3]

In 2001, after Vallas left CPS, Arne Duncan was named CEO. He carried the same neoliberal agenda forward as CEO in his oversight and management of Renaissance 2010 until President Obama tapped him to serve as US secretary of education. Part of Duncan's legacy is the expansion of charter schools that decimated neighborhood schools.

Initially I thought Renaissance 2010 was a terrible joke being played on the city; I didn't believe it would really happen until I started to see it in action. And to be perfectly honest, I wasn't worried for myself because I taught at a selective enrollment school that required testing for admission and would never close—for a variety of reasons. Yet even though I was personally protected, I knew my sisters and brothers throughout the city were being devastated. Renaissance 2010 led to the closure of more than 100 public schools; maligned veteran Black teachers, paraprofessionals, and administrators; and launched so many charter, contract, and alternative schools without unionized workforces.

The devastation felt by the neighborhoods where Renaissance 2010 was implemented needed to be addressed head-on. We wanted our union to testify at board of education meetings and the perfunctory public hearings that were held prior to closing traditional public schools or opening charter schools. We wanted our union to organize massive protests against these policies, but our appeals were ignored. Yet these deliberate attacks on Black teachers, students, and schools moved along without a coherent response from those in the best position to understand and address the problems. When I started teaching, almost half of all

CPS teachers were Black. When I left the classroom in 2010, less than 30 percent of CPS teachers were Black.

It was all frightening. I had to know more, so I started reading everything I could get my hands on about the attacks on public education and the public sphere in general. What all of this meant for those of us who cared about publicly funded, publicly managed public education is that we had to move our union in a different direction. When we started meeting as a group in 2008, we weren't interested in running the CTU. We just wanted a more vigorous response to Renaissance 2010.

The stuff they were talking about doing at that meeting in Pilsen reminded me of my student activism days in the 1960s—I felt like I was right back where I started. It was this full-circle thing. And then we started doing stuff. Jesse Sharkey, Jackson Potter, Al Ramirez, Kenzo Shibata, Debby Pope, Carol Caref, Stacy Davis Gates, Norine Gutekanst, Jay Rehak, George Schmidt, and other refugees from PACT started showing up at public hearings, announcing ourselves as members of CORE (Caucus of Rank-and-file Educators) while denouncing school closings and charter openings. It was exciting. Who ever heard of a caucus that wanted to include the needs of students, parents, and community organizations that worked with young people?

We went to every single charter school opening hearing and every single board of education meeting. According to the rules of the board of education, you could only speak in the public portion of the meeting every other month, so we carefully coordinated our speaking and personal business days in order to have our issues amplified. We'd take a personal business day off from work and go. In those days, the board would call the principals of schools to verify that we hadn't improperly used benefit days and to get a sneak peek at our "grievance." By that time, I was at King and I had a very supportive principal, who didn't mind me taking off time as long as I left stuff for the kids to do. Then we started meeting with other people, going from school to school to try to get more people involved.

It was a hard time for public schools. There was this ugly, nasty, just totally foul conversation going on around schools and teachers and our communities. I think teachers were fed up, and so were paraprofessionals and clinicians. Everybody was. Something needed to change.

Chapter 10

CTU President

In 2010, I was elected president of the Chicago Teachers Union. When Jesse Sharkey and the rest of the CORE caucus started, I had no plans to lead, but I was encouraged to do so. I think people saw that I was smart and had a presence and self-confidence. For years, there was only one main caucus in the CTU: the UPC. The UPC had full support of the AFT. But in CORE, we campaigned. When we ran our election, we had literature, and we went from school building to school building and put our literature in everybody's mailboxes. We organized people to vote for CORE. And it caught the eye of the AFT, whose leadership, including President Randi Weingarten, had collected *alllll* of our mailers and all of our literature. They must have thought, "These people are *for real*."

When we were going school to school and speaking with teachers, I think what resonated most with other members was that we believed in academic freedom and integrity. Teachers we talked with felt overwhelmed by unnecessary paperwork and unhelpful directives about what they had to teach and how they had to teach. When we were campaigning, I went to union meetings with faculty and staff members from many schools, so they had opportunities to see *me* as their possible president. I did a lot of that—visiting and spending time with faculty and staff members all over the city. John was retired by then and he would come with me on all these visits. And he knew everyone. John knew older teachers and he knew younger teachers who had been his former students at Lane. The Lewis name opened some ears to what I had to say. I talked about what we wanted for schools, our members, and our students. I learned from Obama's campaign and election that you have to give people hope. If you don't give people hope, there's no reason for them to shift away from the status quo. Our message resonated with people.

To be honest, I think another reason people relate to me is that I'm a really good actress. For one thing, I've been entertaining myself since I was a little kid. When you're an only child, which I was until my sister was born, you don't have a choice! You have to entertain yourself. So I'd just put myself in the movies, and I liked it so much, I was sure I'd be an actress. I'm not, but what I did—as a teacher and union leader—required the ability to entertain and engage. Then there's my MFA from Columbia College and film and video coursework. I'm a good director, and I also take direction well. I can sit and talk to people. I don't get freaked out when somebody asks me questions because I have answers. I think that's what people see. I want to make people laugh and I want them to have a good time. I want people to be comfortable. Some people think that's a political skill, but I don't think so. What I do think is that it's a skill that translates well into the political arena.

When I was elected CTU president, our beloved union was fractured for a variety of reasons, but our main challenges were the constant turnover of district-level leadership in CPS and the continuing, destabilizing fallout from Renaissance 2010 initiatives—including school closings, school turnarounds, and the expansion of charter schools. This was also the result of what I felt was the hell that Paul Vallas and Arne Duncan initiated and unleashed during their time as CEOs of CPS. Over the course of Vallas's and Duncan's tenure, Chicago became a national leader in corporate education reforms that devastated public schools. This was the era of education reform and leadership that I endured as a teacher. But it was going to be very different to confront the system as CTU president.

At first, the AFT was very wary of CORE. When we won the 2010 CTU election, Randi Weingarten and Mark Richard, her right-hand man and counsel, came immediately to Chicago to see who we were. I called Mark Richard "Mr. Wolf" because he reminded me of the Harvey Keitel character in *Pulp Fiction*. We had a Thai dinner around my dining room table. We had all of our important CORE meetings around my table. Mr. Wolf was sizing us up, trying to convince us of his own movement bona fides ("I worked with Cesar Chavez," etc.), and at the same time trying to figure out if we were going to go on the attack against Randi and the rest of the AFT establishment—if we just wanted to burn the whole place down. They were unsure of us until they realized that we weren't ridiculous. There's this notion that inside every union, inside of every local, there's some outrageous people who have very, very different opinions and views. When they realized we weren't wild, then they wanted to work with us. They saw we had a winning strategy and that the other locals could learn something from us. That was a very profound experience. I knew that AFT leadership would need to take us seriously at some point. Because we *were* serious. Not only did we have a winning strategy, we had a strategy that would work for unions across the country.

§

My first day of work at CTU was Thursday, July 1, 2010. The whole month of June had been very difficult for me. I struggled to adjust to the fact that I was leaving behind one of the best jobs I'd ever had, making a difference in teenagers' lives. As my husband pulled the car off of Lake Shore Drive at Wacker to take me to the CTU offices in the Merchandise Mart, I started crying and said, "Turn the car around. This is a mistake. I have no idea what I'm supposed to do." The only advice Marilyn Stewart, the outgoing CTU president, had given me was, "You don't know what you don't know." Thanks, that was helpful. Let me say for the record, I would never leave our beloved union with my fingers crossed that my successor would fall flat on their face. John consoled me, saying, "You'll be fine, Baby. Don't worry." I relied on him during this time. He would joke that he was prepared to stand in the background. He emphasized that his first concern was always me. I needed to hear this; I was worried.

I felt extremely powerless as a child. And now I was thrust into this position of *perceived* power . . . and some of it was real! It was weird, because along with the power comes this awesome responsibility. And I always felt like I was the least responsible person out of everyone I knew. My husband won't even let me have a dog because he says I'm not responsible enough. While I had no idea what my role as president was, I'd soon find out.

I walked into the office of the president, where the most amazing woman sat at a curved peninsula. Audrey May was the executive assistant to all CTU presidents, from Jackie Vaughn in

1984 to me, with the exception of Debbie Lynch. She had a lot of institutional knowledge. It is Audrey's job to protect the president. On my first day, she could see I was flustered and frightened. Audrey is the picture of a professional and poised Black woman. She was a model in her younger days. She is extremely stylish, very smart, and can be intimidating when she wants to be. Focused and unflappable. She gave me two folders. "This is your mail and these are your appointments." She smiled at me and looked concerned because I'm terrible at hiding my emotions. Then she handed me another folder with a bunch of HR forms. The most important of these included a request for a leave from the board of education—the official paperwork that meant I was out of the classroom. It was real. I was CTU president.

I sat down at my desk, a huge monstrosity that overwhelmed me. I've always liked school supplies, so I checked out the drawers—they were well appointed. Audrey came into my office and asked whether she could sit down. She handed me a binder that had a very detailed plan to include clergy as community partners. The proposal was for a program called PEACE (Parents, Educators, and Clergy for Education). It was clear she was aware of the work the CORE caucus had done to include parents and community in our advocacy. I flipped through the pages and was thrilled to see the highly organized and well-thought-out plan. I asked her, "Whose idea is this?" She made a little gasp, and timidly said, "Mine." I looked at her intently and said, "Then you're in charge!" I thought Audrey was going to start sobbing. Neither of us cried just then, but we probably should have, to release all the tension.

Audrey May is the guardian at the gate, and she became a dear friend. She was the Keeper of the Schedule, and she never allowed people to abuse my time. She would interrupt a meeting and start tapping her watch—a clear signal that it's time for everyone to go. When I got sick, it was Audrey who checked me into the hospital under a fictitious name. It was Audrey who took special delight in telling us how proud she was of our work ethic. The only person who prepared me was Audrey. Audrey helped me.

The racial politics within the union were always extremely present and pressing. Running for CTU president against Marilyn Stewart and the UPC, there was this strong notion that a Black woman needed to be CTU president. That's what people had counted on and why people were looking to me to lead. But in order for white people to accept me—white teachers and white parents—I had to be smart, I had to be articulate, I had to use the "Queen's English" correctly. You know how that is. I did anyway, so it didn't bother me. I had to do it for my job!

I was always very adamant about teaching my children not just chemistry but also standard English, because I knew that they would be judged by how they spoke. My students would sometimes tell me, "Hey, Miss Jennings"—or Mrs. Lewis, depending on when it was—"this ain't no English class." I said, "Your whole life is an English class, so you have to be prepared." I would not let grammar get in the way of my kids. Growing up in Hyde Park taught me that. And my parents were also strict grammarians. They would get on me for saying "ain't," which was a word I loved to say. I loved saying "ain't" because I thought it was very appropriate for what I needed to say and how I needed to communicate. But I also like to joke and play with language. My students told me once, "You are so bougie, Mrs. Lewis." And I said, "Uh-uh! I'm ghet-to, aren't I?" And they fell out laughing. They said, "'Aren't I?'" and fell out! I laughed too. "O-kaaay?!" I'm totally into Lil Jon. I can't help myself. Because

I like a good piece of ignorance. I'm not bougie. I'm a little more ratchet than they know.

As CTU president, I also had to be intentional about my appearance in ways I had never had to before. I had to be out there, in public, and I had to look a certain way. I couldn't just be out there with a fresh-washed face. It just doesn't work like that for Black women. I'm the laziest dame on the planet—I am so trifling. I just don't pull things together well. For instance, whenever I'd put makeup on, it just never looked good, and it was either too much or not enough. I found a woman to do my makeup for my first professional photography piece as CTU president. And I was like, "Damn. I look good. I kinda like that." Eventually, I hired a woman, Denise, to do my makeup. We became close. She really helped me pull things together. She does a good job of making me look very natural, but very pulled together. It's a skill!

Whenever I went out, people wanted to take selfies with me and stuff. I always said yes. The only time I wouldn't agree to it was if I was with other people and they were moving me through the crowd. But when people asked me to take a picture, sure. Still, you have to feel like you're looking good to do that! Because you know they're gonna post it. Black women deal with certain expectations and double standards around appearance. I think of how put together Jackie Vaughn was, her very intentional presentation of self and her beautiful signature hats. She was good at her job, she was sincere, and she was respected. I aspired to that because you have to be on point—it can't be haphazard.

And people can be horrible, particularly on the Internet, with that anonymity, out there sitting in the dark in their underwear typing terrible things. And interestingly enough, online and in other spaces, a lot of the worst things said about me have come from white women who just hate my guts! I would expect it more from white men, who are particularly misogynistic and have this notion that Black women should be quiet. The whole notion of me being an angry Black woman is so funny to me because I'm not angry—"Don't start none, won't be none" is my opinion about a lot of stuff. But I'm not tolerating anybody talking to me crazy. And I think that most people don't understand that, especially white people. Because white people say the craziest shit to one another, and they're never held accountable for it! These people watch way too many TV shows where that's allowed to go back and forth; somebody Black will just pop you one. But there are people of color who will try it too!

I was watching a show on PBS about Black women and mental illness. It was talking about depression and how we don't cope with it appropriately because we're ashamed or because we've been told, "Just give it to God!" I was having this episode where I was really depressed, and I wasn't exactly sure why. And that's why depression, I think, is so hard to deal with: because you can't always pinpoint what it is. And then, in the next moment, I felt like, you know, I'm so happy. I think it's one of those things where you *muddle through*. You muddle through. And we have to give ourselves permission to muddle through, and give ourselves permission to cry, and give ourselves permission to get the support we need.

People don't realize the *stress* that comes with being the front-facing image of an entire union. People would look at me and criticize me and say things about me that were very harmful and hurtful. And I was absorbing that a lot. I don't absorb too much of that anymore. I'm pretty good now at pushing that off. Because I find that's really more about what *those* people are doing and feeling. It's not really about me. One of the best pieces of advice I give people I learned myself from being in the public eye. When responding to the horrible things that people say about you, you need to: *Think* what you want to think. *Write* what you want to write. Just don't press "send." I think you *definitely* have to get it out. If you don't get it out, you'll be crazy. You'll just hold all that stuff in. So get that poison out. But don't feed the trolls. When they get you, go after them—just do it with the edited, redacted version!

§

When I became CTU president in 2010, there had not been a teachers' strike since the nineteen-day-long one Jackie Vaughn led in 1987. There were no strikes during Mayor Richard M. Daley's tenure because he always found funding sources to raise teacher salaries. When a new contract would come out, most people wouldn't read the contract—they'd go to the back pages of the document to see how much money they were making that year. Since we were getting very good raises, nobody was worried or complaining. The other reason there weren't many strikes during those years is because of state legislation. In 1995, the state legislature passed the Chicago School Reform Amendatory Act, which gave the mayor control of the schools and made many items nonstrikable and nonbargainable. That cut down on strikes because Chicago teachers could basically only strike over bread-and-butter issues like wages and benefits. There were many other things that we should have been able to bargain for, like staffing and class size, but we couldn't bargain for them.

In spite of this stretch of years without strikes, the CTU was still very divided coming off the 2010 CTU election. When I became president, there were *five* caucuses running. So my initial goal was to unify factions. We were also in debt when we took over; the CTU had taken a loan from the AFT. People were asking me how I was going to solve all these problems. I would tell them, "Well, my plans are to talk to people and to get people that have those skills together, to come solve these problems. These problems aren't going to be solved by one person with an idea. That's not the way it's gonna work." It's one of those things that seems so basic. I don't understand the logic of not bringing all the interested parties and everyone with ideas to the table. If we're really talking about making changes that benefit everybody, everybody has to be there.

We created a research department and an organizing department. We did not understand how a labor union could exist without organizers. We were moving the union from a service model to an organizing model to empower rank-and-file teachers to do what's best for kids and solve some of the problems in education. As educators, we did not understand how our union could make its arguments without research. So we added a team of researchers to delve into the facts. That way, when the district or the mayor made claims about the budget or about some arbitrary policy, we were able to dispute those claims with the truth. Now, *we* would be the ones issuing reports that the board reacts to—not the other way around.

When Mayor Daley announced he wasn't running for reelection in the fall of 2010, Ron Huberman, then the CEO of CPS, resigned. His background was with the Chicago Police Department, not in education, and he had only been in the role for one year. We didn't overlap much, but I got along well with Ron. He wasn't Black, but I thought he was when I first saw him. I assumed his mother was Black and his father was Jewish. I asked him, "So how come you're so Black?" He said, "No, we're just Israelis." So anyway, Ron resigned, and Terry Mazany, the CEO of the Chicago Community Trust, was made interim CEO until the new mayor could put someone in place. And in 2011, the year after I became CTU president, Rahm Emanuel was elected mayor.

Rahm antagonized us from the jump. His entire campaign felt like bashing CPS teachers. It was as if he were saying this system is bad and all the teachers are dumb. It was the same stuff Bruce Rauner, the Republican multimillionaire private equity manager, who later became Illinois governor in 2015, said—that teachers were "virtually illiterate."[1] Which was so insulting. Not only did Rahm campaign on all of this, it seemed like he wanted to just ham-fist everything. He wanted a longer school day, and he campaigned for it. Rahm had also named Juan Rangel as cochair of his campaign. Rangel was CEO of the UNO charter school network. He was later accused of nepotism, negligent behavior, insider contracts, and other conflicts of interest while managing hundreds of millions of public dollars intended for students. The US Securities and Exchange Commission even brought a federal case against him in 2016 for securities fraud related to the charter schools. Rangel settled, "without admitting or denying the SEC's charges," and paid a $10,000 fine.[2] Corruption and mismanagement in the charter sector was a key feature of the privatization of public education.[3] In the CTU, we were fighting privatization. So Rahm making Rangel a key adviser was another signal to us that an all-out attack on the CTU was about to be launched.

When Rahm was elected, people complained that the city didn't have a Black person in charge of the school district. Rahm brought in Jean-Claude "JC" Brizard, the Haitian American superintendent of Rochester City Public Schools, as CEO of CPS in May 2011. I tried to help JC. I tried to explain to him that the political context in Chicago is very different from the setting he'd just left in upstate New York. I talked to the president of the Rochester local a number of times. I heard JC got run out of Rochester because he didn't understand the context there. I heard he had pushed misguided education reforms like charter school expansion and didn't take the time to get real input or buy-in from teachers, parents, or the community. Teachers in Rochester took a vote of no confidence in his leadership just months before Rahm picked him as the new CPS CEO in Chicago.[4] I told JC, "Look, in Chicago, you need to make alliances with real people, not just the elite. Because the elite in Chicago don't send their children to public schools." I told him he needed to find a different path. And I even gave him what I thought were some good ideas. But he seemed to be enamored of the position. The white folks called him the "premier CEO" because he was always going to the openings of shows or showing up at this, that, and the other thing. It became clear that he wasn't following my advice.

We were also going into a tense round of negotiations over our contract. As soon as we walked in the door as the new CTU leadership in 2010, we received a notice from the law firm of Franczek and Radelet, CPS's outside counsel, that they had a laundry list of givebacks they wanted. They wanted us to give up our contractually guaranteed raise, or they would lay off two thousand school workers. They had a whole chart with different ways to make cuts. The previous administration had convinced them to wait until after the CTU election to deliver this list. In order to get to a reasonable agreement, we reached out to rank-and-file members of the other four CTU caucuses who had run in 2010. We asked them to join us in negotiating with the so-called board of education when, in effect, we were really negotiating with the mayor's office.

In the summer of 2010, we walked together forty-strong as a bargaining unit—which was a big bargaining team—to the Holiday Inn across the street from the Merchandise Mart for a meeting with James Franczek, CPS's outside counsel. It was the first time he had to negotiate with rank-and-file members of our union. Normally, at a minimum, the CTU constitution required that two officers negotiate on behalf of the members, but we wanted to demonstrate a different type of elected leadership. We wanted to make sure that the people who would have to work under the conditions CPS wanted to impose were present. As CTU president, I was trying to make the union more democratic and responsive to our members. You have to give people their *voice* and let them have their say. So I put as many people as I could on the bargaining team, across caucuses and across bargaining units. I wanted to make sure there were counselors, there were nurses, there were substitutes—all kinds of our members. My vision was that everybody needed to be on the bargaining team.

We held trainings for this new big bargaining team. We needed as many of our members as possible to understand that it felt like the board was trying to blackmail us. They wanted us to give back our contractually agreed-upon raises or else face massive layoffs that they were then going to try to blame on us. In these trainings for the bargaining team, we explained how bargaining worked and analyzed the board of education's demands. We even brought someone in to pretend to be a board lawyer to get members used to how things would go in negotiations. I also trained our team on how to enter and exit the room. I had a signal for when it was time to end the meeting. When I slid my chair back, everyone knew to get ready, count to three in their heads, and then we'd all walk out of the room. We had this choreography too. And part of that was walking across the street forty-deep to the first meeting. We took a picture of that and put it on the cover of the September/October 2010 issue of the *Chicago Union Teacher*—the CTU's monthly newsletter—with the headline "Confronting the Board in Force." It was important that we demonstrated a united front because there were attacks coming at us from multiple fronts.

It was already in motion early in 2011, even before he was sworn into office, but Rahm was soon able to shove Senate Bill 7 (SB7) down our throats after he officially took office in May 2011. SB7 steamrolled through the Democratic state leadership in Springfield, pushed by powerful lobbyists from Stand for Children and Advance Illinois (more on them later). Many of the bill's elements were extensions of the Obama administration's Race to the Top initiative, championed by Arne Duncan, former CEO of CPS. It wasn't a surprise that Rahm, also coming out of the Obama administration, supported the bill even before he was sworn in as mayor. The bill curtailed the union's ability to protect our members and allowed for evaluation of teachers based on their students' test scores, an inherently misguided idea. Moreover, it called for layoffs to occur based on those evaluations, not on teachers' experience.

Merit pay could also be based on students' test scores. SB7 made the length of the school day and school year permissive subjects of bargaining, meaning the mayor had the unilateral power to change them. And SB7 also increased the threshold to strike—but only for Chicago!—by requiring that the CTU get 75 percent of bargaining-unit members to vote for a strike. At that time, there had not been a teachers' strike since 1987. SB7 passed the Illinois House and Senate almost unanimously, really demonstrating bipartisan support for the gospel of so-called school reform.[5]

During our ongoing negotiation process over our own contract back in Chicago, the mayor and CPS's bargaining team constantly asked for givebacks. They didn't want to give us any raises and they wanted to reduce our benefits. They hadn't attacked the pension yet, but they said it was coming. The stuff that Rahm said would work better than the "status quo" was still wild—including giving principals more autonomy. I think back on the French program Madame Webster started at Kozminski and my trip to France as an eighth grader. It is a great example of what a strong principal and an innovative teacher can do when they have the autonomy to create amazing experiences for students. Principal autonomy should be used to create great programs and stop the district from doing silly things that don't benefit students. But Rahm's vision for principal autonomy was this kind of absolute power that made people fear losing their jobs if they didn't march to the beat of the compliance drum. It was an even *worse* set of policies because principals just used it to go after people they didn't like, as opposed to people who didn't teach well.

Frustrations were mounting among teachers, so when the 2012 school year came, people just said no!

Chapter 11

Strike!

Our members weren't angry with us; they were angry with the mayor. One of the major issues identified by the negotiating team representing Rahm and CPS was the 4 percent raise negotiated and agreed to by the previous administration—they wanted us to give that gain back to them. We pushed back hard, but little did we know, they would use a clause in the contract to get around this. This clause gave the board of education the option to forgo paying raises if they didn't have the money. Rahm directed the board—unelected and appointed by the mayor—to rescind the 4 percent raise as one of their first acts in office in June 2011.[1] It was a gambit to make our new so-called radical union administration look incompetent. It had the opposite effect; I think it really pushed people over the edge. When I asked previous CTU officers why the article that allowed our raise to be rescinded by CPS was in our contract, they pointed out a clause that said if more money was available, it would be applied to increase raises. Nevertheless, I'd never heard of a time when the board wasn't "broke."

Rahm's rescinding of the raise was a motivating factor in the strike because it immediately made our members suspicious of anything the board wanted; that has never changed, even to this day. As president, I felt supported by this large contingent of members who had their eyes on every piece of language presented to us. There was constant talk of "weasel wording" that allowed the board to get away with what members perceived to be contract violations. The strength of the rank-and-file members was that they seriously questioned the intentions of the people on the other side of the table.

And the questions rank-and-file members asked were informed by their lived experiences and work on the ground in schools. The counselors provided examples of not being able to function as counselors to traumatized students because they were busy with paperwork for special education meetings or coordinating the enormous amounts of standardized testing that provided no help for students. Many of these counselors were also their school's case managers, so this paperwork problem was also caused by the board of education's failure to adequately staff schools. The social workers shared how their working conditions did not allow for the privacy to appropriately help their students. Librarians and arts teachers talked about being taken out of their programs to cover classrooms for absent teachers because the board didn't provide enough substitute teachers. The lawyers looked as if they couldn't believe a word we were saying.

Our educators were sharing up-to-date, on-the-ground situations and speaking from the heart. It was the first time in history that the CTU took rank-and-file members into a negotiating session. In fact, they had originally told us that we couldn't do it. Our chief negotiator was Robert Bloch, from the firm of Dowd, Bloch, and Bennett. He told us that the board couldn't technically limit the number of people we brought to negotiations. I wanted to have three hundred, but settled for seventy-five. The board agreed to having forty of us in the room at a time, but we also had alternates who came to all our meetings and were ready to tap in for negotiating sessions as needed.

Between the nasty and demeaning tenor of conversations about public education at the time and the fact that we were new leadership, I think they just thought we were stupid. After SB7 passed, Rahm was so certain that we wouldn't be able to strike. Because of SB7, a successful strike now required that 75 percent of your people support it. Jonah Edelman, one of the architects of the bill and an ally of Rahm, said: "The unions cannot strike in Chicago. They will never be able to muster the 75 percent threshold necessary to strike."[2] Based on what I knew about the sentiment among our members, I wasn't that worried about getting a 75 percent strike vote. From what I heard, Rahm mistakenly thought that everybody could vote for or against a strike. But no. If you're not a union member, you don't get a chance to vote. It seemed that Rahm had incorrectly assumed that Teach for America—I call them Teach for A Minute—teachers and non-union members would have a chance to throw off the balance. But that's part of being a union member—you get to vote. Matter of fact, we had a whole lot of people sign up to be union members, and then they voted to strike!

We had been organizing well in advance of the 2012 strike. One-on-one conversations with people were a priority. We had a very strong, trained core group of delegates. One of the things we first started offering on a regular basis was more delegate training. In previous administrations, we used to have one big workshop meeting annually. It was sort of like a party at a downtown hotel, and you'd go to a workshop or maybe you wouldn't. But when we came in, we started actually having training sessions for people that were based on organizing principles—very Saul Alinsky-ish. You know? If it ain't broke, don't fix it. Certain things do work!

Negotiations between unions and management should be like negotiations in any relationship. They can and should involve actual relationship building and honest attempts, on each side, to understand what the other side hopes to accomplish. Unfortunately, we live at a time when some politicians and members of the ruling class see us as indentured servants, not public servants. They truly believe we don't do good work and have contrived a variety of ways to prove it. Fortunately, our union has fought consistently for fairness in the workplace. One of the reasons I was attracted to teaching was that I knew my paycheck did not depend on whether my boss liked me, the color of my skin, or my gender. I knew that the man down the hallway didn't make more because he was male or white. Our union had long ago negotiated a salary schedule based on years of experience and educational attainment. I thought it was terrific that if you loved teaching and didn't want to go into administration, you could still make a good living. I found it despicable that politicians and corrupt charter school operators could attempt to make the public hate us.

A lot of people doubted that students and their parents would support us in a strike. I even remember that one of our people was upset that data showed the average teacher in CPS made $75 thousand. She said that our students' parents don't make that kind of money, so why would they be sympathetic to us? I countered that the relationships we built with our parents were much deeper than our quest for raises. We asked for changes in working conditions that would benefit our students—their children. Parents understood the need for smaller class sizes, librarians, arts teachers, counselors, and social workers. Most of our parents knew and understood that all of us had degrees, including our paraprofessionals, who needed at minimum an associate degree. They clearly understood that there was a correlation between education and wages, which is why they trusted us with their children every day. It's why we fought for their children to have a quality education as the foundation for their future success. And while arguing for educators' needs, we also contended that our parents deserved to earn a living wage too.

Parents and communities rallied around us because we talked to them constantly. We explained what was going on in schools. There's not a single parent in the city who doesn't believe that their children should have a smaller class size. Even though, with the laws at the time, we couldn't bargain for it, parents wanted that for their kids. Parents wanted more transparency around what goes on with the board. And they had been so mistreated by the board themselves. Some parents thought they could just go in and talk to the board, especially the more privileged parents who weren't being affected by school closings or things like that. They got the same basic "Thank you, goodbye" that other parents were getting. I think that was an element of public support for us too—the board treated parents terribly.

We invited parents to be a part of our process and give us ideas about what we should bargain for, even though, by law, we couldn't bargain for a lot of things. But the fact that parents wanted to be there, and that they felt comfortable with us, was an accomplishment. When we first got into office, I would meet parents on missions to lobby legislators in Springfield, Illinois, the state capital. At first, when I would introduce myself and say that I was the president of the CTU, they didn't want to have anything to do with us. But when we started centering parents' values and their issues in our messaging and advocacy work, they started to treat us very differently. We weren't just looking at bread-and-butter issues, we were talking about root causes, and I think that was different for a union. And we were trying to embrace community issues along with the ethos: If we do well, you do well. It's just that simple.

One of the advantages that CORE had, which none of the other CTU caucuses had, was this kind of community support. We had already built *relationships* with community organizations. We had relationships with the Kenwood Oakland Community Organization (KOCO), a decades-old grassroots Black Civil Rights organization in my own neighborhood. We had relationships with Brighton Park Neighborhood Council (BPNC), a community-based social justice organization in the predominantly Latinx Southwest Side. We had relationships with Logan Square Neighborhood Association (LSNA), a long-standing community-based organization serving the Latinx community in the Logan Square neighborhood. We had relationships at Community Organizing and Family Issues (COFI), a parent-empowerment organization made up of primarily Black and Brown mothers and grandmothers. I was starting to build relationships at Raise Your Hand, a parent advocacy organization that, at the time, included more affluent parents fighting against standardized testing. I kept running into them when I had meetings with legislators in Springfield. Raise Your Hand was very standoffish at first. They would say, "We don't really want to be involved with the union." So I would tell them, "We all have the same goals!" Our relationship with Raise Your Hand also grew over time.

The result of all these relationships was that when we were at the negotiating table, we had rank-and-file educators with us and we had parent and community support. Parents and community groups were fed up with the state of public education. They were fed up with Rahm Emanuel too.

§

As we say in Chicago, "Politics ain't beanbag, baby." As a matter of fact, it's hardball. And Rahm and I had our battles. One of my proudest moments came during contract negotiations in 2012, when educators on our team said they wanted time to read the contract. We listened and honored their requests, but Rahm was trying to rush us into settling the contract and moving forward. The CTU House of Delegates voted to extend the strike by two days to allow members to read the contract before voting on it. We decided to extend for two days because extending for only one day would make the vote fall on Rosh Hashanah. I said, "Rahm, you're a Jew. It's Rosh Hashanah!" I remember him telling me he could get *fifty* fucking rabbis to come in here and tell us why we should just go do this. I told him it was *awful* of him to say that. "I'm going to shul, thank you very much," I said to him. "Now, you can take your soul and do whatever you think you need to do with it." He was furious. We regularly had these kinds of exchanges. I don't know who he thought he was.

Every time Rahm tried something crazy, I'd say, "I'm from Chicago. You aren't. You're from Wilmette, buddy. And you grew up *very* differently from the way I grew up." Even though someone could look at my resume and think I grew up cloistered, I did not. My parents were *real*. That's one thing I like about Black parents. Black parents are *real*, and they don't take any shit off their kids. People can look at my resume and see that I got the best of everything—training, education, exposure—the whole thing. But I was grounded by the experience of being raised by Black parents. Don't get it twisted! But Rahm had no clue. He was just looking at my resume.

The disrespect, Rahm's constant condescending, dismissive tone—none of this helped him at all. I had dinner with him early on, as he was transitioning into the mayor's office. I was trying to get to know him and build a relationship. As I recall, it was at dinner that he told me that 25 percent of kids in our schools were never going to amount to anything and so he wasn't going to throw resources at them. That's how he saw our kids! That's how he talked about our communities! Of course, he denied he said any of this when asked by the media. And he tried to come for me too.[3]

He should have known it wasn't going to work. I had read Shirley Chisholm's book *Unbought and Unbossed*. I loved it. Then I got a Shirley Chisholm Award from the City College of New York, which meant so much to me. I *so relate* to the sentiment. I *am* unbought. There's not enough money in the world to buy me. Well, there is. I have a number. But it's $10 billion. I joked with Rahm once and said, "Get your boy Ken Griffin [Republican billionaire] and Michael Sacks [Democratic multimillionaire] together. I'm sure you can come up with $10 billion. Because that's what it would take. Everybody has a price? That's mine." It would have to be enough money so I could give at least half of it directly to teachers and bypass the board of education because those bastards would misuse it. Isn't that some ignorance? That's a good piece of ignorance. Rahm did not actually try to buy me, but I wanted to make it clear that I would remain unbought and unbossed. All jokes aside though, there truly is not enough money in the world to make me turn my back on kids.

When Rahm cussed me out at a meeting at his office in the summer of 2011, I *knew* he was going to come at me like that. So I was prepared with what I was going to say in the room and how I was going to be publicly outraged about it after the fact. We were meeting about his plan for a longer school day, which I didn't agree with because, to me, his plan for a longer school day was more of a babysitting plan to warehouse kids. He got upset, pointed his finger at me, and said fuck you to me.[4] I wasn't going to have him talking to me like that, so I cussed him out right back. I didn't care about him. He was disrespectful, but those exchanges didn't bother me. I didn't know how long he was going to be mayor, and I didn't know how long I was going to be president of the union. But if we got off on a foot where he thought he could just say anything he wanted to me, I knew that would be bad for my members and our schools. And that I *did* care about.

Later, I talked to Maxine Waters about it. She told me that he always talks that way to people. I couldn't believe she would tolerate that shit! I remember when I heard that Rahm said something shitty to Danny Davis, the long-standing Black congressman from the West Side. This was before I was union president, when Rahm was still in DC as chair of the Democratic Congressional Campaign Committee. I sat across the aisle from Danny Davis on a flight from DC to Chicago. I said, "Congressman, are you OK?" Because he was looking all down. And I remember him telling me that he was fine, but he had to deal with this Rahm Emanuel. Rahm had set an amount of money every congressperson had to raise. Congressman Davis told me that he told Rahm that his constituents didn't have that kind of money. That he couldn't just get that kind of money from his constituents. And Rahm told him he didn't give a fuck about Davis's constituents—that was the number. This is how he talked to people. This is how he tried to talk to me too, but I wasn't going to have him talking to me like that.

He'd made a huge tactical error because he thought I would keep quiet about his disrespect. Instead, I went *right* to the press and told them what he had done. I told the media that I didn't appreciate the way that he talked to me, that my father and husband never talked to me like that, and that it was immensely disrespectful to me and CTU educators.[5] He thought I wouldn't tell anyone about all the crazy stuff he said to me because that's the way things are done. People in power are used to doing stuff in back rooms, and I don't work like that. I said, "Listen, I'll take my earrings out, and put the Vaseline on, and we can go to blows!" I wasn't having that fool talk crazy to me! And I think that shocked him. Based on his response, I think he was actually surprised. But I been knew Rahm. And with guys like that, with bullies, you always have to put them on blast. If you don't, they get away with murder. And they will *continue* to get away with murder.

Rahm didn't want negative attention. What you have to remember is that Rahm is not an ideologue, he's transactional. If you remember that about Rahm, then you can put all things in perspective. Now, if being around *you* can help him do some shit *he* wants? Then he'll be around you.

In my mind, it's all about birth order. Rahm is a middle child. He's got his older brother, Zeke, who's the doctor—he's the smart one. He's got his younger brother, the baby, Ari, who's the cute one. And then there's Rahm—not as smart as Zeke and nowhere near cute as Ari. He's *such* a middle child. His brother Zeke's book, *Brothers Emanuel*, is really good. It's very insightful. And you better believe that I read that muthafucka with a fine-tooth comb. Because I was kinda like, "I need to better know who I'm up against." That was something my first husband had taught me, back when he encouraged me to read Ayn Rand. Opposition research: know your enemies.

Another way that Rahm underestimated me is that I don't believe he thought I was a *real* Jew. But the thing is, if you're a real Jew, you must understand the roots of Judaism. Sometimes I think Jews who are born Jews don't always understand that Judaism is rooted in social justice. All you have to do is just read Torah. They say things like, "There shall be no needy. No man should be hungry." Especially at Passover, you're supposed to invite the stranger into your home and share Seder with them. You know, to me, that is the root of social justice.

And on top of everything else, Rahm doesn't seem to have any problems talking crazy to people he doesn't know. To me, that is absolutely the biggest no-no. I was surprised he didn't learn *anything* from being around Obama. But Rahm is a trip. When I got sick and had a stroke, all of a sudden, he *likes* me. Who's sending me matzo ball soup from Manny's Delicatessen? Rahm. Because he knew I would take my members out on strike again. I'd strike his ass in a heartbeat. I would organize every member I had to walk the streets again and close the city down, if it was about fighting to do the right thing for kids. Bring all the parents with me. We had done it before, we could do it again.

§

In 2012, Chicago teachers and paraprofessionals were fed up. It had been nearly twenty-five years since the CTU last went on strike. For decades, the mere memory of past strikes was enough to make the board bargain seriously at the table. By the end of the 2011–2012 school year, the state of negotiations—as well as the daily disrespect the board showed educators—demonstrated that faded memories would no longer suffice. Even if 75 percent of our entire membership voted for a strike authorization, as SB7 required, that did not guarantee that we would walk the picket line. In fact, at the time, we thought a strike authorization would lessen the possibility of a strike because simply demonstrating our level of unity might cause the board to see reason. Striking was our option of last resort. Yet we also knew that in the past, when all teachers, paraprofessionals, and clinicians banded together in solidarity, it led to increased power, protections, and safeguards that were essential to the well-being of teachers and students in our schools.

But the CPS CEO, Jean-Claude Brizard, and the mayor wanted educators to engage in a sort of "learned helplessness," a condition in which a person learns to behave helplessly, even when the opportunity is restored for them to avoid an unpleasant or harmful circumstance to which they have been subjected. According to psychologists, this condition results from the perceived absence of control over the outcome of a situation. I told our members, "Don't fall for the 'okey doke'!" Together we had the power to change the outcome of how the board treated us and what they could do to our students. We knew the power was in our voting hands and marching feet.

In February of 2012, the CTU issued a report, *The Schools Chicago's Students Deserve.*[6] The report offered ten recommendations for strengthening neighborhood schools and addressing inequities in the school system. It recommended reducing class size, providing wrap-around services for students, and giving greater access to pre-kindergarten and full-day kindergarten to make sure students got off to a good start. These were educator-backed and proven reforms. Unfortunately, members, parents, and our students were all vulnerable to what we perceived to be the haphazard policymaking of the unelected board of education and CEO Brizard. The district spent millions on unnecessary testing and politically connected charters and turnarounds. At the same time, they refused to access available local tax increment financing (TIF) surplus funds that could have alleviated budget pressures. Instead, CPS continued to use general state aid—that was supposed to fund instruction—to pay off their debts. On top of that, they wanted to reduce our pay and benefits, increase work hours, and meddle with our pensions. I promised my members that as long as I was president of the CTU, our research would continue to expose the lies, expose the political agenda around education that had absolutely nothing to do with education, and change the narrative.

Educators were tired of feeling blamed, bullied, and belittled by the very district that should have been supporting them. The same twisted narratives about us that Rahm had campaigned on were part of a broader national conversation about schools. As teachers, it was like we weren't being heard. And the only way anyone in power talked about improving conditions in schools was to create more charter schools. How were they closing schools and yet opening new schools at the same time? It wasn't logical. It didn't make sense. Charter schools weren't unionized, and they could (and did) hire unqualified people to teach for two years and then kick them out. In the charter model, teaching became a temp job. They're not there long enough to make the relationships, to see how a family works over time so that they can bring more than just content expertise into the system. This work is about how we develop human beings and the love of learning. What kind of system has teachers coming in, and then two years later they're gone? That's not sustainable. That made veteran teachers—who had been teaching for years or decades and valued the training, the craft, and the profession—pretty angry.

We lived in a city that no longer viewed educators as important, trustworthy resources, essential to helping our youth develop values, skills, and the knowledge required for them to enter adulthood as thinking and engaged citizens. We lived in a city that had done everything it could to take the joy out of teaching and learning. Teachers were being deskilled, unceremoniously removed from the work of governing their schools, and reduced to technicians and babysitters. We were being asked to work harder and longer in order to inflict mindless experiments—which the school district tried to call reforms—upon our students. We saw this as having nothing to do with our children and more to do with real estate transactions and rewarding politically connected charter operations with school buildings. But when the experiments failed, it was teachers who were evaluated and blamed. Experiment after experiment after experiment. Did we not learn anything from the Tuskegee experiment?! But whose children did they experiment on? Ours. And is that OK? No!

The schools were moving to longer school days and a longer school year—without any commitment from the district to give students and teachers the resources they needed. I did an interview with *Democracy Now!* where I explained our concerns about these changes:

> We know that quantity is not quality, and from the very beginning, we didn't actually fight [Rahm] on this longer school day because the law gave him the opportunity to impose it. But we wanted to make sure it was a better school day, and a better school day for us included a

> broad, rich curriculum for our students. We were concerned that the direction of school reform is about standardized testing, so it's about [long blocks of] math and reading all day, which doesn't engage children. [. . .] We wanted to make sure they have art, music, PE, world languages. These are the kinds of things that also stimulate critical thinking, and we wanted to also bring the joy of teaching and learning back into the classroom.[7]

Instead, the board said it wanted to lengthen the school year, cut professional development days, decrease pay and benefits, and evaluate teachers based on student test scores. The board wouldn't even explain to the public how it was going to pay for a longer school day and year!

In all my twenty-two years of teaching, I had *never* seen a climate as hostile to students and educators as the one created by Rahm Emanuel, his handpicked school board, and his handpicked CPS leadership team. We wanted what was best for the more than 400 thousand school children who we were honored to teach and to support—and we were prepared to fight for them. So we went on strike to fight for the type of schools we knew our students deserved. Rahm had told me that 25 percent of our children would never amount to anything, so why should he give them anything? Well, he picked the wrong fight, and he was about to find out what fighting for that 25 percent looks like. We were fighting for the heart and soul of public education.

In June 2012, we took a historic strike vote—one they said we'd never be able to win. More than 90 percent of our members voted and, of those who voted, 98 percent voted yes. Our solidarity made a mockery out of the union-busting SB7 and its 75 percent strike authorization threshold. That July, an independent fact finder sided with the CTU during contract talks and upheld our positions opposing a longer school year and longer teacher workday. The rest of our "negotiation summer" was spent preparing our members for a potential work stoppage. We spent those months training our delegates, energizing our members, and preparing for the inevitable. The board's refusal to take our concerns seriously led us to issue a ten-day strike notice on August 22. And on September 10, twenty-nine thousand strong took to the streets, and Chicago experienced its first teachers' strike in twenty-five years.

When I was a little girl, I used to enjoy the days when I could catch a ball game with my father. Whenever a baseball player would knock the ball straight down center field or hit a powerful home run, Dad would lean over and say, "Wow! He just made a believer out of them all!" That phrase always made me laugh as I watched the player round his bases, though as a young kid, I didn't really know what it meant. Looking back, that was Dad's simple way of saying that if the other team didn't think their opponent came to play to win, they were sadly mistaken. There's something to be said about underestimating your opponents. Bullies take joy in knowing that their acts of cowardice are at the expense of people they see as weaker or inferior to them. Their faith in terror tactics is only shattered when the abused stand up and will take no more.

And that's what happened when members of the strongest teachers' union in the country went on strike for seven days in the fall of 2012. We refused to be bullied by CPS any more. We showed the board, city hall, and their well-financed surrogates that we intended to fight for our profession and for our students. Even when we disagreed on things internally within the CTU, externally we stood united and strong. The board did not believe that our members would stand up for what was best for our children. The board did not believe that parents and community members, whose sacrifices mirrored our own, would support us. On September 10, 2012, we made believers out of them.

They were wrong. Truth triumphed over lies. Justice prevailed over injustice. Solid research exposed a million inconsistencies. Organizing and communicating directly with those most impacted by education policy—students, teachers, and parents—defeated misinformation campaigns and anti-teacher propaganda. Democracy looked like a sea of red walking strong in the streets of Chicago. Democracy sounded like the voices of teachers, paraprofessionals, and clinicians unafraid to speak up for themselves and our students. Even Brizard had to acknowledge this. Reflecting on the strike in a 2013 interview with the Fordham Institute, he said: "We severely underestimated the ability of the Chicago Teachers Union to lead a massive grassroots campaign against our administration. It's a lesson for all of us in the reform community."[8]

People across the globe took note of our struggle because so many had lost faith that our voices could be heard over the noise of Wall Street and the so-called school reformers. Reporters converged on Chicago to share our stories. Thousands of dollars poured into our solidarity fund from around the country. Rank-and-file members became the new heroes of the labor movement. People from as far away as Denmark, France, London, and South Africa were asking us how we did it—meaning how did we accomplish so much when we were considered underdogs in the fight? We called out the people who claimed we used poverty as an excuse, but always made excuses themselves for not challenging poverty. The people who willfully or ignorantly supported policies that destabilized communities were called on the carpet.

Chicago had become the epicenter for the education justice fight in America. All eyes were on us. I was proud that our members chose to work together, picket together, march together, and make their voices heard together. They were inspired and invigorated.

And as we knew they would, our local community supported us. Under CORE's leadership, the union's image had improved. In addition to strengthening our organizing department, we strengthened our communications department in August 2011. In a poll, 74 percent of surveyed Chicago voters had favorable opinions of public school teachers and 55 percent had favorable opinions of the CTU.[9] The media finally had to listen to us. Journalists started taking a critical look at many of CPS's claims about charter performance and the impact of disastrous school closings on our communities. Newspaper editorials and commentaries started to reflect CTU research on issues of poverty, class size, and school privatization. Even the anti-labor *Chicago Tribune* had to take time off from their attacks on us to admit that Chicagoans now sided with teachers on just about every issue relating to our public school system. We made sure that our rank and file were front and center in the press. We gave teachers, paraprofessionals, and clinicians media training. They told our stories; they spoke our pain.

When CORE took the job leading the union in June of 2010, none of us had ever been union bosses before. We had expectations of our team, but we didn't really know what to expect. We were bound to make mistakes and stumble. And we did. When we were elected, we knew we had yet to face the hard part. The four of us who were officers at the time—Jesse Sharkey, VP; Kristine Mayle, financial secretary; Michael Brunson, recording secretary; and me—were committed to doing the job with all our might. It was hard to stand in the place of leadership, particularly at a time when so much was at stake. It ain't no crystal stair.

So what was the catalyst for our transformation from a do-nothing union to a do-something union? What moved us from a place of fear and complacency to become a leading voice against misguided education reform? Ralph Waldo Emerson said, "Nothing great was ever achieved without enthusiasm."[10] So that's what we did. We came with enthusiasm and put our whole souls into it.

Lois Weiner writes about this in her book *The Future of Our Schools*. As she explains it, just as there is no escape from building the union at the base, there is no getting around the hard work of developing authentic alliances with parents and community activists. These are important coalitions that acknowledge historic inequalities and support communities in their needs, rather than paper organizations that are dusted off when the union wants to displace community support.[11] This was the new CTU. We were the national model for teachers' unions around the country.

Frankly, in 2012, we *won* many of the things we fought for. We stopped the worst of the attacks, but not all of them. No contract will be 100 percent perfect, and we did have to make some compromises, but our campaign was successful. We maintained our salary schedule, stopped merit pay, and got protections against dramatic health cost increases. Beyond bread-and-butter issues, we also won gains for students: guarantees from the district that students would have access to textbooks on day one; that CPS would add six hundred new art, music, and world language positions to provide our students with a well-rounded, enriching education; and that social workers and counselors would have access to private spaces to serve students. In a broader way, in the face of coordinated pushes for privatization, the strike also changed the conversation in Chicago and nationally about public education by advancing issues like class size, school funding, facilities' needs, and working and learning conditions to the forefront.

Of course, CPS didn't keep up their end of the bargain, but we also hadn't been on them about it. You have to hold their feet to the fire. That's the one thing I know about the Board of Education of the City of Chicago—they will not do the right thing, if given any other options. They spend more time trying to figure out how they can get around stuff in the contract than anything else. From what I heard, CPS even convened principals for a big training to show them how to get around stuff in the contract. They spent time doing this, instead of showing them how to work with teachers and adhere to the contract so they don't get in trouble. In the months after the strike, contrary to what conservative pundits and members of the media would have had people believe, I was not roaming the countryside looking for robber barons to maim and kill. We had to get right back to work to enforce the contract and fight school closings.

We knew that the battle for the 2012 contract was not the end of our work; it was the beginning. We expected a wave of retaliation, and we expected the board and city hall to try to save face by continuing their assault on teachers and on neighborhood schools. The impact of this assault was profound and damaging.

§

A few weeks after the strike, CPS CEO Jean-Claude Brizard resigned. It was reported in the media as a "mutual agreement" between him and the mayor. But it seemed to me that Rahm fired

JC.[12] JC was only in the seat for seventeen months. Rahm then brought in Barbara Byrd-Bennett as the next CPS CEO. She was a veteran educator and administrator who had previously held top district leadership posts in Cleveland and Detroit. We got along. Two middle-aged sisters, you know? People speculated that she was brought to Chicago specifically to close schools because she had presided over school closings before—in Cleveland, with an unelected school board, and in Detroit, where the state had taken over the schools.

CPS's plans for another large round of school closings went public not long after the strike. In February 2013, the board of education announced the 129 schools on the year's hit list for closing. By throwing around big numbers—first 330 potential schools in December 2012, and then backing down to 129 in February 2013—it created dual scenarios of shock and false understanding. They were trying to shock us with a ridiculously high, completely unrealistic figure, then show how much they'd heard our cries when the final tally was considerably less. Members of a commission appointed by the board to consider school closings felt CPS didn't have the capacity to close more than 100 schools, and said that attempts to close even a fraction of that would be a disaster. Even before the final list came out at the end of March 2013, we thought that the final number would be closer to fifty—and that was still fifty schools too many.

However many closings they attempted, we knew it would be billed as CPS "listening to the people" and "taking community input into consideration" in making its final decision. "We heard your cries," they would say before trying to sell us forty to fifty closings as a show of sacrifice and "tough decisions" that had to be made. It was all rhetoric we'd heard far too many times before. Our message to our members and to community members was to continue to build power—if your school is not on the list, fight for your brothers and sisters who are. We had to try to keep that fight alive, stay active in the media, and urge aldermen and legislators to take the fight up the ladder.

What angered me the most was how the board invented a crisis by repeating lies and toyed with the emotions of hard-working and dedicated parents, teachers, students, and staff by making them fight publicly for their schools. In 2013, CPS claimed Chicago had lost around 145,000 school-age children since 2000; this figure included all children from birth to age nineteen living in Chicago, even if they'd never attended CPS schools. They claimed an incredible loss when, actually, CPS lost closer to 35,000 students during that time.[13] Considering the exodus of more than 200,000 people from Chicago, mostly African American, due to the demolition of public housing in places like the State Street corridor and Cabrini-Green, one would expect the loss to CPS to be much higher. But, at that time, it wasn't.

CPS claimed to operate with a "growing billion-dollar deficit," yet had more than a $500 million surplus in the early 2010s. They claimed to have no closing list or plan toward the end of 2012, yet the press reported on an internal CPS document from September 2012 with covert plans to close or consolidate specific schools, and on CPS's dog and pony show of "engaging communities" in these decisions.[14] CPS removed 201 of 330 schools from the closing list based on community input, but many removed were charter schools, which were never going to be shuttered; they had five-year contracts that CPS could not break. By the winter of 2013, they were allegedly working with the community to reduce the list of 129 schools for a surprise reveal in March. But it certainly seemed that CPS officials and Rahm already knew what the final total would be. They had known it for months.

That spring, in talking to our members, I harkened back to Lani Guinier's three questions: Who made the rules to the game? Who are the winners, and who are the losers? What are the stories the winners tell the losers to keep them playing the game? If the status quo is maintained, our children and our members will never be winners because the game is rigged against us. Children of the elite are given a full, rich curriculum that allows them to explore, create, and imagine, while the children of the poor and those who chose publicly funded public education are assigned the drudgery of test prep. Children of the elite are given a curriculum that prepares them to rule, while our children are given a curriculum that prepares them to be greeters at Walmart. Whenever you hear "It's for the children" or "We'll provide a high-quality education," remember that these are pretty words to keep us complacent and in the game. That's why we have to change these narratives.

We reached out to the community to advise us on how to help them in their struggles to protect their neighborhood schools. We had fifteen diverse community-based organizations that we worked with in the Grassroots Education Movement (GEM). GEM was an alliance of community organizations, parents, teachers, and unions fighting together for education justice. We held meetings, workshops, and forums with parents and community organizations. We rallied and protested with people who were fighting against the closure of their neighborhood schools. CPS held hearings out in the community for each school that was on the list. The meetings were wild. Hundreds of parents, students, and community members were bussed into each of these meetings, along with folks from GEM and CTU organizers. Thousands of people were coming out to defend their schools. And we continued to call for a moratorium on all school closings.

At the end of March 2013, the district released the list of the fifty schools they planned to close. Their plan would affect nearly 50,000 children and threaten the employment of approximately 1,300 teachers, clinicians, and paraprofessionals. It was clear that this would have devastating consequences on our communities—particularly Black communities. Neighborhood schools are community anchors, where veteran educators know and teach several generations of the same families. And many of those educators may have attended the schools they worked in. It had been the same for me. Even though there were never any openings in what I wanted to teach at Kenwood, it had been my dream to teach at my old high school, and I did do my student teaching there. And I knew from personal experience that school closings create conflict and traumatize the kids who experience them.

My first experience with a school closing was when I was a kid at Kozminski. When I started eighth grade in 1966, the board of education opened the new Kenwood High School in the building that had previously housed Kenwood Elementary School. Afterwards, they split up and transferred the 500 or so Kenwood Elementary students to three different elementary schools in the area—what we would now call receiving schools. Around 100 of the kids were sent from Kenwood Elementary School to my school—Kozminski. Unlike today, school closings were rare back then because there were so many kids—they needed the buildings. And I came up in the era of "Willis Wagons," the mobile classroom trailers brought in to accommodate overcrowding and keep Black kids segregated. So, at thirteen, I didn't really know much about school closings, but I do remember when the Kenwood Elementary School kids showed up at Kozminski, people said that if your school had to close, it must be a bad school. That's what I heard, even though that's not why Kenwood Elementary closed.

Scattering kids across multiple different elementary schools set up conflict and culture clashes. I can't remember her name, but one new girl who transferred to Kozminski from Kenwood Elementary was so mean and nasty to our classmates that one day I just asked her, "Why are you acting like such a bitch?" Her response to me was, "You just called me a bitch—I'm going to kick your ass!" I was confused because I didn't call her a bitch; I'd asked her why she was acting like one, and I thought that was significantly different. But I was ready to go. When I went home for lunch—because you still could go home for lunch in those days—I told my grandmother about it. She rubbed Vaseline all over my face and said, "She will try to scratch your face because you're so pretty."

Needless to say, I was ready for the big fight. School let out at 3:15 p.m., and that's when all the storm clouds gathered. I got the first punch in, and she never did hit me. But she leaned forward, grabbed my little white blouse, and snatched it open, popping the buttons and exposing my bra to all the little boys in the circle. I was humiliated. It was embarrassing enough to be in a fight, and my good punch to her face was for naught. I grabbed my books from one of my friends and headed home. As I left, I shouted, "You really are a *bitch*!"

What I didn't think about at the time, and what I know now, is that it must have been extremely difficult for that girl to start all over in eighth grade at a new school. She had to build new relationships with teachers and students from scratch.

How traumatizing it must have been for her to have her old school close.

When political leadership and CPS green-lit school closings, they began with a vengeance. All those memories came flooding back—my humiliation and the recognition that children from different neighborhoods were being forced to begin again, go to brand-new schools together, and do this without preparation for conflict or culture shock. This is one of the reasons why I've been opposed to school closings. It's *visceral*, because I went through it myself.

I had also seen the effects of school closings in the more recent past. When we were starting to organize CORE in 2008, we railed at the board against closing schools. Between 2001 and 2008, almost sixty schools were closed.[15] Through the Renaissance 2010 plan, many of these schools on the South and West Sides were turned into privately managed charter schools and others were converted to district-run schools with new admissions criteria. But some of the closed buildings just sat empty. And some kids got lost in the shuffle. The impact of these school closings forced children to cross dangerous gang lines.

One of the highest profile and most tragic incidents related to these school actions on the South and West Sides was the murder of Derrion Albert in 2009. In 2000, CPS CEO Paul Vallas decided to phase out George Washington Carver High School, a neighborhood high school on the Far South Side, and convert it into a military academy over the course of several years. Carver was founded in 1947 to accommodate families and students living in the Altgeld Gardens public housing complex, built near the school a few years earlier. Fenger High School became the zoned neighborhood high school for students who lived in Carver's old attendance area. But Carver and Fenger are five miles away from each other! So kids had to cross multiple neighborhoods and gang lines to get to and from school. It caused serious problems, ultimately contributing to the highly publicized and brutal videotaped murder of Derrion Albert, a sixteen-year-old Fenger High School student, in September 2009.[16] It was a terrible tragedy. Unfortunately, similar conflicts and disruptions played out at different levels across many school communities and neighborhoods that experienced school closings and other school actions during the "school reform" era of the 2000s and 2010s.

A few years later, I did an interview with *Dissent Magazine* where they asked me about the connection between violence and school actions. This is what they published, and I stand by it:

> Chicago has a very different gang structure than most other cities. We've got a lot of Capulets and Montagues. There's no hierarchy. In Chicago, this block may be fighting against the next block. And they're not just defending drug territory. They're defending respect. Because our children have so little of it, if somebody disrespects them, it escalates outrageously. Part of the problem is that we don't have counseling programs for children early enough. [. . .] Some of the conflict resolution that you should learn in play has disappeared. In Chicago, we have issues of safety and a murder rate that is out of control. Think about Hadiya Pendleton, the young woman who was murdered after she'd performed at Obama's inauguration. She actually went to the school where I taught before I left the classroom, and I knew one of the kids that was involved in her killing. In Chicago, this stuff touches everybody.[17]

In May 2013, the board of education voted to close nearly fifty schools—at the time, the largest mass closure of public schools in modern US history. At the board meeting, before this vote happened, I told the board: "I personally feel that you are on the wrong side of history, and history will judge you." They did it anyway. Of the schools impacted by this round of closures, 90 percent had majority Black students and 71 percent had a majority Black teaching force. Students with disabilities were also disproportionately impacted.[18] When Rahm presided over this mass closing of schools in 2013, I called him the murder mayor. Chicago's murder rate was high. But Rahm also murdered schools by closing them. He murdered jobs. He murdered housing. Our communities were suffering.

But the 2013 round of school closures was also different from previous rounds of closures in important ways. As I explained to *Dissent* at that time: "In the past, when school-closing hearings took place, maybe ten or twelve people would show up. We're now getting thousands of people to come to those hearings. And what they are saying with one voice is, 'Keep your hands off my school.'" The groundswell of parents, students, teachers, and community organizations that supported the CTU strike, fought the school closings, and demanded a different vision for the future of public education had changed the conversation about urban education. The CTU was a movement, and we refused to let the discussion of urban education and the related issues of racism, housing, poverty, and unemployment continue to be ignored.

There was certainly more work to be done. As I told *Dissent*, "When you're playing on somebody else's turf, you don't have control. So the key is to change the rules of the game."[19]

Chapter 12

The Fall of the So-Called Reformers

After the 2012 strike, the power of our union was known nationally and around the world, but this global acclaim belied the reality of how difficult our work was at home. I had no idea how tough it would be to fight off the constant beat of the right-wing agenda. Frankly, they had a twenty-year head start. When Mayor Daley took over the schools in 1995, he installed a CEO. That already told us what direction the schools were going in—a business model. The business model does not work in education. The business model does not work in public spaces. The market approach to public education tramples on democracy. But business and corporate leaders—Democrats and Republicans—were the ones driving the education reform agenda. The people who got to have the loudest voices in the conversation were the people who knew the least about education. They'd spent more than twenty years convincing the American public that our nation's teachers are lazy, stupid, and impossible to fire. These lies have been oft repeated and take so much time and energy to refute.

For example, if you believe the corporate education reformers, it takes five to ten years to get rid of a bad teacher. First of all, what is a bad teacher? Second, tenure is simply a guarantee of due process, not a job for life. This protects teachers from arbitrary actions, as people should not be able to simply walk into classrooms and say, "You're fired!" without allowing educators opportunities to defend themselves. And while the anti-union refrain is "Tenure is a job for life," the general counsel of the CTU, Robert Bloch, was shocked when he discovered how easy it was to dismiss a tenured teacher.

But that's the gospel of "school reform." First, fire teachers. And when you lose money, don't fire them on the basis of seniority, fire them on the basis of a new evaluation tool that judges teachers by students' test scores—a ridiculous instrument that has nothing to do with reality. We have to use the proper tool for the proper job, and tools designed to assess children cannot be used to assess their teachers. The tests we were using for students really were not even good at assessing the children! You can't use a knife to get a nail or a screw out of a bracket. You need to have a screwdriver. Oppressive testing mandates and the high stakes attached to them make it difficult to focus on real education. This is why we had to resist the continued assault on publicly funded public education in Chicago and across the country. Politically, the right-wing agenda went too far.

Why are these lies so common and so widely believed? I think it's because everyone has been to school, and everyone had at least one teacher they didn't like or click with. And if everyone went to school, then everyone is also an expert on school, right?

In addition, there are those Programme for International Student Assessment (PISA) tests that American students seem to do so poorly on, year after year. What most people don't know is that the United States tests all of its students, not just selectively, like some other countries do. If you factor in poverty, we score closer to the top in reading, science, and math. Furthermore, American students have always scored in the middle of the pack. But out of the blue, in Ronald Reagan's first term, the US Department of Education released *A Nation at Risk: The Imperative for Educational Reform*—a report that labeled America's public schools as failing and the worst in the western world. Big lie. The language in the 1983 report was so alarmist: "Our Nation is at risk. . . . The educational foundations of our society are presently being eroded by a rising tide of mediocrity that threatens our very future as a Nation and a people. [. . .] We have, in effect, been committing an act of unthinking unilateral educational disarmament."[1] Then in 1987, William Bennett, Reagan's secretary of education, had the nerve to call CPS the worst school system in the nation.

What struck me about that charge was that CPS at that time was led by a Black superintendent, Manford Byrd Jr.; the city had a Black mayor, Harold Washington; Black teachers outnumbered white teachers; and there were a significant number of Black school-based administrators, as well as a Black presence in the bureaucracy at central office. On top of that, Jackie Vaughn was president of the CTU at the time—the first Black president of the CTU. So this major national attack on public schools was launched specifically at Chicago during this time, and it felt particularly racist to me. Bennett's poor assessment of CPS schools was also duly noted by the powers that be in the city. Shortly afterwards, the "city fathers" hatched a plan to rid CPS of Black people—leadership, faculty, staff, and students. It wasn't announced, and it took them years to ultimately execute.

But this refrain that schools were failing and only business or corporate leaders and ideas could save us became ubiquitous in Chicago and nationally—across political parties—in the years to come. It guided the Civic Committee of the Commercial Club of Chicago—types who pushed charter schools and concocted Renaissance 2010 in the 1990s and 2000s. It was a bipartisan effort, touted locally and nationally by Democrats and by Republican "reformers," like Bruce Rauner, who emerged from this milieu and ran with this agenda once they were in power.

§

Bruce Rauner, the eventual Republican candidate for Illinois governor in 2014, launched the most heinous and self-righteous attacks on public education. He denounced public unions while pocketing millions of dollars managing public workers' pensions in his private equity firm. As an adviser to Rahm Emanuel, he had been an architect of SB7, the 2011 legislation that undermined educators' seniority and raised the threshold to strike. Rauner noted that he shared Rahm's vision for education: "On school reform we see things the same way. [Rahm] believes in charter schools and competition and choice . . . which I am a definite believer in." Rauner has donated millions of dollars of his personal fortune to charter schools and has a school in the Noble charter network named after him. Rauner and Rahm had a long-standing relationship. They vacationed together in Rauner's multiple luxury homes across the country. Before Rahm became mayor, Rauner had made millions of dollars with Rahm when they worked together in the private sector. As a Democratic strategist described it, "they are cut from much of the same cloth."[2]

Rauner basically bought the 2014 gubernatorial election, powered by a personal fortune that he poured into expensive TV ads.[3] The sitting Democratic governor, Pat Quinn, was sweet and kind, but hapless. Quinn chose Paul Vallas, corporate school reform darling and ruiner of the public school system, as his running mate. Quinn had made it his "life's mission" to fix pensions. You can imagine how well that sat with the labor community. With the choice between Quinn and Rauner, a lot of Illinoisans either bought into the rich man's "I'm one of you, and I'm going to 'shake up' Springfield" pitch, or they sat out the election, fed up with the nonchoice between the lesser of two evils.

I had first met Rauner in 2010, when I was introduced to him by one of the pastors of a megachurch on the city's South Side. The pastor had run afoul of the previous CTU president and our membership by calling us the equivalent of an infamous murderous drug gang. He wanted an opportunity to make amends, and I wanted a rich benefactor to subsidize a form of professional development called Lesson Study. Rauner was—and still seems—convinced that CPS teachers are subpar. While he was governor, one of his old emails from 2011 resurfaced where he referred to CPS teachers as "virtually illiterate" and CPS principals as "incompetent."[4]

Knowing that Rauner had some pull in the education reform community, I accepted the pastor's invitation to meet with him. Audrey May accompanied me to the high-rise paean to naked capitalism that was his two-story office, right across the street from the Merchandise Mart where the CTU main offices were then located. We were ushered into a large conference room with very comfortable-looking chairs around a large and long table. I sat down in the first chair I came to, but Audrey quickly ushered me out of that chair. "Never sit with your back to the door in an office where you don't know the person," she said. "Sit on this side, so that when he comes in the door, you're looking at him." Chalk up another great piece of advice from Audrey. Frankly, it was a great power move.

About five minutes later, Rauner sauntered in, looking every bit of the hedge-fund homey that he is. He spent some time discussing his background—he had gone to public school in the suburbs. He sounded like a typical middle-class kid who made good. He told me how at one time he supported National Board Certification, a rigorous and highly respected professional certification for teachers. I knew about it, as I am a National Board Certified teacher. But in his estimation, it was not producing results fast enough. So Rauner wanted to look at systems, not individual teachers. I approached him with the idea of funding a system-wide professional development program called Lesson Study. He asked me what Lesson Study was. I looked at him incredulously. "So let me get this right. You are the head of the Education Committee of the Civic Committee of the Commercial Club of Chicago and head of the Chicago Public Education Fund [a private education funding organization that uses a venture capital model], and you've never heard of Lesson Study?" He actually smiled amiably, instead of sneering. He shook his head. I peered intently across the table. "Do you think the system of education in Japan is good?" He allowed that he thought it was amazing. "Lesson Study," I poked him, "is the system of professional development in Japan. You just said you thought they had a good educational system. Why not help bring that here?" I thought it was a perfect opportunity to segue into policy talk.

By then, the pastor had arrived at the meeting, and our conversation went down a different path for a while. Then Rauner finally settled in and told me casually that he and I probably didn't agree on much. He told me that he didn't believe in communal anything, but we had something in common; we'd gone to the same school. Now it was my turn to be incredulous. I knew he hadn't gone to Kenwood and he couldn't have gone to Mount Holyoke, but not willing to let him get to me, I asked, "Where was that?" "Dartmouth," he said proudly. That was before I knew he had his name plastered on several buildings. "So what class are you?" I was doing the math in my head, thinking he was from the class of '68 or '69, and with a straight face, he looked at me and said, "Class of '78." Now I was taken aback because I thought he looked so much older than I did. "I'm class of '74." He said he knew because he looked me up in the alumni database.

It taught me a lesson about always knowing who I was meeting with. A quick Google check usually does the trick! I politely got up and told him I was looking forward to working with him in the future. Little did I know he would bankroll and directly support what I thought were some of the most regressive, aggressive tactics designed to undermine Black educators and, by extension, Black students in Chicago. Nor did I have an inkling that he had political ambitions. Oy gevalt!

Once he was in the governor's office, Rauner launched his Turnaround Agenda, which included working to make Illinois a right-to-work state (right to work for less, I say) like our surrounding neighbors, Missouri, Michigan, Indiana, Iowa, and, most notably, Wisconsin. He expressed open admiration for Wisconsin governor Scott Walker, a Republican who basically eliminated public workers' collective bargaining rights and drastically cut spending on public services, including education. These actions led to massive protests by Wisconsin teachers and public workers in 2011, when they occupied the state capitol for multiple days. Rauner also envisioned and promoted an end to collective bargaining in Illinois, which unions knew would ultimately lead to collective begging. He also had a great time using certain people who had made careers out of championing the education of Black children. They shall remain nameless because they are shameless, and I don't feel like getting into a public fight with those folks. They know who they are. People who've been around Chicago politics for a long time told me they'd never seen so much cash on the streets. Unfortunately, the collective pocketbooks of the so-called powerful special interest unions couldn't compete with the hedge-fund machine that felt like it was printing money and dropping it into Rauner's accounts.

By 2015, with Rauner as governor, the neoliberals were in control of the executive branch, turning Illinois decidedly purple at a time when public unions were under a full-frontal assault. Rauner immediately went to war with AFSCME (American Federation of State, County and Municipal Employees); he walked away from contract talks when they wouldn't accept a pay cut and a huge increase in their medical contributions. He couldn't go after CTU directly, but it seemed he wanted to punish us for going on strike in 2012, so he used his friends in the right-wing stink tank—the Illinois Policy Institute—who occupied a significant number of his senior staff positions.

§

It took me some time to realize that people who truly believe they are doing good work, maybe even God's work, do a lot of evil in this world. When I think back to my first years as CTU president and the conversations during the debates over SB7, the collection of so-called education reformers formed a rogues' gallery, composed of central casting characters, that made this time feel like a very long *Twilight Zone* episode. Of course there was Bruce Rauner, who I already discussed. But there was also R. Eden Martin (the president of the Chicago Commercial Club and a partner at a top law firm in the city) doing his very best Montgomery Burns impersonation, Robin Steans (a millionaire heiress, charter school founder, executive director of Advance Illinois, and former teacher—we actually taught at Sullivan at the same time when I was at the beginning of my career), and Jonah Edelman (the CEO of the national corporate reform group Stand for Children—I call them Stand *on* Children). They all exhorted politicians to enact the law.

During the "negotiation" of SB7, the other side of the table included the CPS labor relations department represented by Rachel Resnick, former principal and general company girl who led the district's labor relations office, and Joe Moriarty, one of their top labor relations attorneys. Our side of the table included Dan Montgomery, newly elected president of the Illinois Federation of Teachers; Audrey Soglin from the Illinois Education Association; and Mike Persoon, an attorney and partner at Despres, Schwartz, and Geoghegan who was managing our lawsuit against the board of education based on what we argued was a racist school turnaround policy. We wanted to make certain that nothing in the new state law would affect our lawsuit. In retrospect, we should have also had our own labor lawyer there, but we were inexperienced. Our legislative director had no access to the General Assembly leadership, and neither did our outside lobbyists. So we were left to negotiate vigorously on our own.

I recall that in those conversations, Robin Steans used a tired trope of a social studies teacher who didn't know that the weather did not continue to get hotter as you moved south of the equator, a fact that many people who've never studied geography might not know. She was arguing that this person should lose their job for that. We're talking about a teacher losing a job, losing a home, their child possibly having to come home from college, because Robin Steans is an arbiter of what good teaching is? She taught history at Sullivan High School when I also taught there. When we were at Sullivan, I found her to be distant, cool, rigid, and relatively uninterested in the goals of the school.

As she sat across from me years later, discussing this bill and her views on teachers, touting her ed reform bona fides, I found myself seething. Steans and her cohorts brought up all the lobbying firms to pass this heinous piece of legislation. As I sat across the table listening to her sanctimonious drivel, I had to be restrained by Audrey and Dan from jumping across the divide and screaming. I knew it would not help me or my members or, more importantly, the children of Chicago.

There is something wrong with people who simply cannot hide that they feel superior to others. During the lead-up to the strike in 2012, Steans got on television, on *Chicago Tonight*—our nightly local PBS news show—and expressed how disappointed she was in the CTU for not being "reasonable" and following the law the way she intended it.[5] I'm like, "Who the fuck are you?" I was thrilled when I heard she was going back to managing her family's foundation instead of continually dipping her toes into education policy. But I should have known better. She continues to be deeply involved in shaping education policy as the executive director of Advance Illinois. She taught for a short few years, and now she's an authority on education policy. It must be nice to be a dilettante. Winning the womb lottery is something most of us simply don't have access to. I will give her credit for sending her children to CPS—I'm not sure whether they went all the way from kindergarten to twelfth grade—but at least she had some real experience as a parent.

Jonah Edelman's participation in all of this was particularly odious and discouraging to me because his parents, Marian Wright Edelman and Peter Edelman, a Black woman and a white man, had been serious civil rights advocates. I felt Jonah had crossed a very bright line. I watched the YouTube video of Jonah Edelman at the Aspen Ideas Festival in 2011. He was boasting to the audience how, with Advance Illinois and Stand for Children "working in lockstep," they had suckered us into this bad bill. He made clear that it was all about union busting: "With Rahm Emanuel's involvement behind the scenes, we were able to split the IEA [Illinois Education Association] from the Chicago Teachers Union." They made big campaign contributions to show that they "could be a new partner to take the place of Illinois Federation of Teachers—that was the point." He bragged about how they funded lots of lobbyists: "We hired eleven lobbyists, including the four best insiders and seven best minority lobbyists, preventing the unions from hiring them." They had the political will and ability to "jam this proposal down [the unions'] throats." And if they could do it in Illinois, then they could do this kind of school reform anywhere: "Our hope and our expectation is to use this as a catalyst to very quickly make change, similar changes, in very entrenched states."[6] They were doing real dirt. And Edelman made clear how all these people were connected, coordinated, and working together with him: Bruce Rauner, Robin Steans, Rahm Emmanuel, and billionaire Ken Griffin.

Ken Griffin, the richest man in Illinois at the time, seems like a real villain, though I've never met him in person. Griffin's hedge fund, Citadel, has been mentioned in several national articles and in Michael Lewis's *New York Times* best-selling book *Flash Boys*, about how Wall Street and the market are rigged. During the conversations around teacher evaluation within CPS, some of the "city fathers" convened a meeting in downtown Chicago that also included some Harvard researchers. I was told that during that meeting, several people asked what the teachers thought about it and inquired how the district might tailor the evaluations to the needs of the teachers and students. I heard that at that moment, Griffin got up and abruptly interrupted the speaker, saying something to the effect of: What are you talking about? Just grab something off the shelf and cram it down their throats! And if I ever had the chance to get Griffin, Jonah Edelman, and all these people in the same room, I would have sat down and said to them, "I know you have the *best intentions*. I know you have the best intentions. But you are FUCKING SHIT UP!"

These are the people who we were actually fighting against. I think the problem is that most people have no idea about who the power is behind the throne, so to speak. Like Bruce Rauner. Before he became governor, nobody really knew who he was. But he was doing all kinds of gamesmanship behind the scenes before he broke out politically and ran for governor. With Penny Pritzker, it was the same thing. The billionaire Hyatt Hotels heiress and charter school advocate funded Stand for Children, advocated for SB7, and chaired Obama's fundraising committee, and then Rahm appointed her to the Chicago Board of Education. Later, Obama appointed her as the US secretary of commerce. I got trotted out to meet all these people within the first six weeks of being in the job as CTU president. It was dizzying.

When I spoke at the City Club of Chicago after the strike in 2012, someone asked if I'd prefer that corporate leaders sit on the sidelines instead of trying to make schools better. I said that I thought these wealthy "reformers" should do what they do when they donate to the Lyric Opera. They don't give money to the Lyric and then go tell the singers how to sing. Where is Andrew Carnegie when you need him? Leave it alone. Give your money and walk away, buddies. When you don't know something, don't dilettante your way into it. We needed business leaders who would work with us and our schools to create engaging, vibrant environments for students and their families, not corporate dilettantes only looking to serve their own interests.

§

These Chicago experiments with privatization, "school choice," high-stakes testing, and accountability soon became national policy. During his first term, President Obama appointed former CPS CEO Arne Duncan as his secretary of education. In my opinion, Arne took the damaging policies he implemented in Chicago under Renaissance 2010 with him to the national stage, where he rolled out Race to the Top as the new federal policy for education nationwide in 2009. Race to the Top would in effect dismantle neighborhood schools and open new charter schools, over-rely on standardized tests to judge students and teachers, and privatize and make schools compete for limited public funds. If you are competing for crumbs, what are you getting?

As was the case in Chicago and Illinois, at the national level, there was also bipartisan support from Republicans and Democrats for these corporate education reform policies that prioritized competition, school closings, charter school expansion, and a reliance on standardized testing tied to new accountability measures. As I said in an interview on *Chicago Tonight* in 2013, "accountability is a word that gets pushed around and means a lot of things. But what we found in Chicago, by and large, it means punishment." And there is nothing transformational or visionary about that.[7] Barack Obama, a Chicagoan and the first Black president in the United States, ran on a platform of change in 2008. But with his education policy—Race to the Top—he largely just extended and elaborated on George W. Bush's No Child Left Behind and Chicago's Renaissance 2010. Teachers paid attention to this.

Barack Obama won reelection in 2012, but many teachers, paraprofessionals, and clinicians who had voted for him, canvassed for him, and cast ballots for him four years earlier didn't go the extra mile, because he had turned us all off with Race to the Top. While Obama didn't go as far as supporting vouchers, he did advocate for charter schools without a scintilla of real evidence that they work. I think he was under the influence of the marketing, the so-called 100 percent graduation rate, the miracle cure that doesn't exist. He supported the testing regime that we all despised. We'd hoped the president would come to his senses and find ways to give all children the kind of education his beautiful daughters got at the Lab School in Chicago and Sidwell Friends in DC—fully resourced, elite private schools. If we'd seen that, we would have known there were real commitments to education, justice, and equity. Unfortunately, that is not what happened. In Chicago, the expansion of charter schools further undermined existing public schools.

"School choice" is a misnomer. When you look to market solutions for public schooling problems, you prioritize the level of the individual over the common good—it becomes just about what my individual kid needs. Not what's good for all kids, just my kid. If you are competing to take the best-prepared kids out of neighborhood schools, then who gets left behind? School choice—through the expansion of charter schools, selective enrollment schools, and magnet schools—created a tiered system that decimated neighborhood schools and exacerbated inequities across the school system. We documented this in a 2012 CTU report: "Huge resource disparities proliferated—selective enrollment schools, turnarounds and charters received state of-the-art facilities, equipment and supplies, while neighborhood schools serving low-income students of color deteriorated. These disparities, supposedly established to give 'choice' to parents, reflect a two-tiered system akin to what is commonly understood to be apartheid." And the school closings that accelerated during the corporate era of school reform didn't help. "Overall, students have not benefited from school closings or turnarounds. Despite the illusion of 'choice,' students affected by school actions have most often landed in schools that struggle as much as their previous school." Corporate school reformers promote the idea of choice, but these are false choices that don't serve all students, particularly not our most disadvantaged students.[8] We knew we had to defend the common good of publicly funded, publicly managed public education.

One of the reasons we decided to unionize the charter school teachers and staff is because once you unionize charter schools, it makes them less palatable to people who want to destroy public education. In the 2017–2018 academic year, most charter schools' staff were still not unionized, but the Chicago Alliance of Charter Teachers and Staff (ChiACTS) had made inroads in organizing members at several charter schools and had about one thousand members. That year, after much debate and discussion, a significant majority of CTU members voted for ChiACTS to merge with the CTU. When charter teachers had the right to strike, they did.

The next academic year, there were *two* charter school strikes—the first in the nation!—which *shocked* me. I didn't expect them. Because charter schools have such high opinions of themselves, like they're doing something so wonderful for the kids. It's very missionary-like. And they like to think that they're *so* different from us. Yet they have the same kids and the same issues. As I told the *Chicago Tribune* in 2017, "It's the management companies we have the issues with, not the charter teachers, not the students, not the parents."[9] But without a union, they have no due process. That's one thing that's uniformly sad about charter schools. And once they got due process, the teachers seemed to understand why they needed it. Because their administrations were just willy-nilly firing people, hiring their friends and their friends' children—which was something that did go on back in the day, decades ago, in the public schools too. Back then, if you didn't belong to the Democratic Party, you weren't getting hired as a teacher in Chicago. It was a patronage job, like all the other ones. Eventually, we started to see the tide turning against charter schools.

Our movement was shifting the narrative! When the NAACP issued a resolution calling for a moratorium on charter school expansion and strengthening of oversight in governance and practice in 2016, it was a huge reversal. For years, chapters of the NAACP had supported charters and helped them secure lots of funding. The language of the new resolution was striking because it so strongly reflected the arguments that the education justice movement had been pushing for years—including CORE and many of our community partners. It stated:

WHEREAS, charter schools have been a rapidly growing sector of the education system, increasingly targeting low-income areas and communities of color; and

WHEREAS, charter schools with privately appointed boards do not represent the public yet make decisions about how public funds are spent; and

WHEREAS, charter schools have contributed to the increased segregation rather than diverse integration of our public school system; and

WHEREAS, research and reports have documented disproportionately high use of punitive and exclusionary discipline in addition to differential enrollment practices that violate protections of student rights for public schooling; and

WHEREAS, research and civil rights organizations have documented violations of parent and children's rights, conflicts of interest, fiscal mismanagement, and psychologically harmful environments within several rapidly proliferating charter management organizations; and

WHEREAS, analyses of annual missing charter funds have been estimated at nearly half a billion dollars nationally; and

WHEREAS, researchers have warned that charter school expansions in low-income communities mirror predatory lending practices that led to the subprime mortgage disaster, putting schools and communities impacted by these practices at great risk of loss and harm; and

> **WHEREAS,** current policies force district campuses to accommodate co-locations of charter schools, resulting in shortages of resources and space and increasing tension and conflict within school communities; and
>
> **WHEREAS,** weak oversight of charter schools puts students and communities at risk of harm, public funds at risk of being wasted, and further erodes local control of public education; and
>
> **WHEREAS,** the NAACP shares the concerns of the Journey for Justice Alliance, an alliance of 38 organizations of Black and Brown parents and students in 23 states, which has joined with 175 other national local grassroots community, youth, and civil rights organizations calling for a moratorium on the Federal Charter schools program, which has pumped over $3 billion into new charter schools, many of which have already closed or have failed the students drawn to them by the illusive promise of quality.[10]

For a respected legacy civil rights organization like the NAACP to reverse their position like this was really significant. The NAACP changed their stance because the charters didn't live up to their lies. You can't fool *all* the people *all* the time. The marketing schemes don't always work. I never trusted the line that charters pushed, that they could do what we did, but better and for less. The only *less* was that they paid their teachers less!

Before long, charter schools started pushing for equal funding in Illinois, so they weren't even actually claiming that they could do it for less anymore. They were saying that they needed the same amount of money *plus* unlimited support through fundraising. With no oversight. And then some of these schools were keeping the money allocated from the state and CPS per student, even when they expelled or pushed students out of their schools. One thing we wrote and made sure to include in the charter bill we drafted and pushed in 2014 is that the money follows the kid. And charter advocates were like, "Well, suppose a kid comes from CPS and comes to our charter school?" And I said, "Well, then you get that money." I don't have a problem with that. But when you start kicking out kids? You don't get to keep the money—sorry! You kicked the kid out, and that kid is coming back to *our* district-managed public school. That money needs to come back too. We knew the charters were also using these hyperpunitive and exclusionary disciplinary measures to make money—they were fining the kids, holding them back a year, and doing all this kind of wild stuff. And we're the ones—the CTU—that exposed that with our research.

That's why I tell people all the time, you can't do organizing work without researchers. And you can't rely on other people to do it for you, either. How many unions have research departments? Every place I go, I tell them, "You have to have the research, and you have to have the internal organizing." CTU had *no* organizing department and *no* research department until CORE was elected and we created one. Since we've established one, unions across the country have taken our research report, *The Schools Chicago's Students Deserve*, and made it their own. It's been appropriated for their local context, and I think that's a good thing.

The narrative was changing. Despite what the corporate school reformers might suggest, as educators, we were the education experts. We had ideas and solutions to address problems in education and we offered to help. But if they tried to push us aside and dismiss us, we were not going to go quietly into that good night.

§

I have three questions that I always ask when faced with decisions surrounding the work we do—does it unite us, does it build our power, and does it make us stronger?

Before I was CTU president, it just never dawned on me that people who are good trade unionists might not know how to really do member engagement. It's not a given. I think that a lot of leaders don't trust their members, first of all. This is not hard to believe, quite frankly, because a lot of members have these wild ideas and wild notions, and they want you to drop everything you're doing and do their thing instead. But there's a process. If you want to do that, you have to go through a committee. Make your appeal to the committee that would do that—it might be human rights, might be women's rights—whatever your idea is, put it to a committee. And then the committee will recommend it to the executive board. And then the executive board will recommend it to the house of delegates. That's how you get stuff done within a union.

The first time I really realized how important the CORE victory in 2010 was for other unions was when we went to the American Federation of Teachers conference that summer in Seattle. At the conference, all these people from unions across the country kept coming up to us and telling us how much they were inspired by the way we fought back against the pervasive negative narratives about teachers and public education at the time. These national relationships with other teachers' unions were important. I had a good relationship with Alex Caputo-Pearl, who was elected president of United Teachers Los Angeles (UTLA) in 2014. LA is the second largest public school system in the country—behind New York City, but larger than Chicago. Caputo-Pearl is a former history teacher, and he's actually a very good guy—we had a *lot* of conversations about the strike. He wanted to understand how we pulled it off. And I said, "Man, you've gotta organize. Not just your members. You've gotta organize the public. And you've gotta *really* organize the parents, who are gonna be mad with you because they have to figure out what to do with their kids during the strike." And I told him to keep an eye on external organizing. "One of the things that's problematic is people are always trying to bring new people in," I said. "Man, you've got to organize the people you *have*." That's what we call member engagement.

I think leadership, in general, is hard. You have this responsibility for all these people, which also means you have to be able to get along with politicians who really control your destiny. So you can't go in and just piss them off. Because that's what our members would do. Our rank-and-file membership is ready to walk into somebody's office and just cuss 'em all out! You can't do that. You have to figure out, too, where people are. And then you have to meet them where they are and *take* them to the next level. And *that's* what we do as teachers. That's what differentiated learning is about. That's what we do, and we're good at it. You have to do the same with your members and in the political space.

The wave of teachers' strikes that took off in 2018 across the country—#RedforEd—was wonderful. It was happening in Republican-led states or states where teachers didn't even have the *right* to strike—in Arizona, Oklahoma, Kentucky, West

Virginia. They went out anyway. Those teachers hit the streets in right-to-work states. Because you can't pay people $39,000 a year to cover how hard the work of teaching actually is. For one thing, everybody's going in their pockets to buy supplies. I know I never spent less than $300 per semester out of my own pocket when I was teaching. One of the things we had to bargain for in our contract was an *increase* in the supply money from $100 to $250. I just think people don't *realize* what this work entails! You know, they really think we're *lazy*, that all we do is go down to the teachers' lounge and sit there and kvetch. And we do that, too! But it's not all we do. It was really important that when those teachers protested in the wave of Red for Ed strikes, they were wearing *red*—CTU red. It wasn't a coincidence. The CTU inspired other teachers across the country to fight against austerity budgets and for our profession and what our students deserve!

I see political bravery in unions today. I've been thinking about what it means to advocate for someone other than yourself. The key to the survival of teachers' unions is that they provide powerful pathways to success for educators, students, and our communities: (1) we have to reclaim our profession, (2) we have to advocate for social justice (housing justice, economic justice, racial justice), and (3) we have to organize for good working conditions because, as we know, our working conditions are our students' learning conditions. It is imperative we see the three interconnected elements as components in a larger vision of educational justice: where our schools are equitably funded and resourced, where our students come to school and can walk there in safety, and where our schools are adequately staffed with school nurses who can take care of health needs, social workers who can provide appropriate therapeutic sessions or referrals, and counselors who counsel, not do mounds of paperwork. All of these issues are inextricably linked.

The skills we have as teachers are so applicable in other areas. I think that's another reason why I'm so disgusted by rich people who look down on us because we chose this public service *and* we chose to work with poor Black and Brown kids. They don't appreciate the skills we really have. They've come up with this idea of testing us to death, thinking that these tests will even out the disparities (that exist because of poverty) because they've bought into the "poverty doesn't matter" group. No—poverty matters. When I hear the word "grit," I'm already thinking, *mmmmm-nah*. It's a visceral reaction. Because these kids already have grit in order to make it through their daily lives. They *have to* have grit. If grit's all it took, they'd be the highest achieving out there.

The conversation about grit also emphasizes individual achievement above the common good, evoking school reformers' market-based logic. "I'm a self-made man. I pulled myself up by my bootstraps." How many times have you heard that? But no one does anything alone. No one. No one pulls themselves up by any bootstrap. You didn't do it all on your own. A parent, a grandparent, a relative, a teacher, someone in your community played a role in your life. Some ancestor who you will never know prayed for you and wished upon a distant star that you'd be right here where you are right now. Everyone needs someone along the way. And our children need all of us—the community, the collective. But we live in times with people who believe that the market is always right and has a solution for the problem, no matter the evidence to the contrary (*cough, cough*, 2008 crash?!). In the fight for public education, we have to push back against this logic. This is why in the CTU, we work with our communities and bargain for the common good. We struggle together. We celebrate together. We must live in this place together.

No other profession has a responsibility as great as those of us whose primary job it is to teach, to inspire, and to motivate young people whose lives are rooted in systemic poverty. Students living in or experiencing childhood poverty are much more likely to face significant unaddressed obstacles to classroom learning than their middle- and upper-income counterparts, and this impacts educational outcomes. In fact, research shows that family income is the most significant predictor of academic success among students in the United States.[11]

We can't fix what's wrong with our schools until we are prepared to have honest conversations about poverty and race. We don't like having those conversations because they make us uncomfortable. But until we do, we will be mired in the no-excuses mentality—that poverty doesn't matter. Poverty matters a lot when you are teaching children who you know are in survival mode and distracted by their lives, because they may not know where their next meal will come from or where they will sleep that night. Poverty matters a lot when you are teaching children who have seen and are experiencing trauma that so many people can't even imagine—levels of trauma that most people cannot recover from without intense emotional support. Poverty matters when children of middle- and upper-class parents have access to therapy, but our children have no resources or supports to address the violence they see and experience. And then we punish those same children with restrictive discipline policies and school reforms that don't actually help them.

We need to be forcing the discussion about poverty every time they want to force the discussion about school reform. The fat cats don't understand what it means to go to school hungry or walk through neighborhoods riddled with violence. Corporate school reformers focus a lot on accountability for teachers and principals. But where is the accountability upward for the hot mess they create for the rest of us? Who is held accountable for exploiting and destroying neighborhoods? Who is held accountable for the lack of stability in the city, which has lots of other implications? They don't understand that these schools, the buildings where we teach, are safe havens for so many of our students—it's where they find the support they need.[12]

When you're doing stuff for the right reasons, I think it's easier to do it. And I think that's the reason why the education reformers had to regroup, starting in 2012. They haven't gone away, but they're a lot quieter. People thought that Rahm was going to come here and fix everything, because he knew all these rich people—Rauner, Griffin, Steans, etc.—and they were going to help him fix Chicago. But none of them dug in their pockets for any of the projects that we really needed.

It doesn't matter what new initiatives CPS concocts from year to year in the silo of CPS, without any stakeholders at the table, if there are no ways to adequately fund them. Chicago has to end its addiction to tax breaks and find ways to generate revenue for our schools. We need to fully fund the schools our students deserve. This is what makes the privatization of education so terrible and wrongheaded. Our communities do not lack inspiration, they lack revenue. And we can't talk about the budget for schools without talking about revenue. We must get creative about it—looking at TIFs and financial transaction taxes, getting out of toxic swap deals, exploring new forms of progressive revenue at all levels of government. If we were at the table when it was time to talk about the CPS budget, I'd have more to say about revenue. But we never were. City leaders responded to people with deep pockets, while parents, teachers, and community folk were left out of the process of governance and decision-making. What would it look like if we had leadership that was inclusive of other people and if we really worked together?[13]

Chapter 13

A Life Well Lived

I decided to run for mayor because people asked me to. It's one of those things—when called, you have to serve. It was the same thing when I ran for CTU president. But when I did run for union president, and we won, I saw what an impact it made on the entire city. So when people asked me to run for mayor, I said, "OK. What's it going to take?" People were saying to me, "I will collect signatures for you. I will do this. I will do that." And they did! That's how Harold Washington ended up running for mayor in 1983 too—and became the first Black mayor of Chicago. People asked him to run. He got picked. So I felt like, "OK. I will do it."

Angela Davis is my idol, you know. Barbara Ransby, who is a professor at the University of Illinois Chicago, had us speak together at the Freedom Dreams conference she hosted at the university in May 2014. Another one of my heroes, Robin D. G. Kelley, was also there. Angela and I were talking backstage. I just wanted to touch her. She had been an inspiration to me since my student activist days. I said to her, "You made my life what it is." She was so nice and loving and generous of spirit.

I told her that I was being pushed to run for mayor, and she said, "Well, Karen, if they're asking you to run for mayor, you have to, you have no choice." Our conversation is the reason I decided, finally, to run.

What I found interesting—and a bit surprising—during my very short-lived run is that there isn't really any consensus Black politics in this city. People were willing to fight for what they wanted in their communities, but I didn't see a united front or a coordinated, coherent agenda. In fact, folks seemed a little frightened of everything. Maybe it's the fact that people are struggling for crumbs, because when you're dealing with austerity politics and it's about survival, people are just climbing over each other. So it was scary to me when people would tell me that they saw me as the future of Black politics in the city, scary because I didn't feel very political. But there I was, stepping into the political arena.

I based my mayoral run on education, the economy and jobs, health care, and housing—*especially* housing. All these issues are more connected than people want to believe. I talk about this stuff all the time and how all these things intersect. And if you don't pay attention to these details, you get lost in the struggle. Part of my task during my run was to help people understand how all this stuff intersects.

I was looking for models of how to govern differently and I wanted to see how Chokwe Lumumba's version of democracy worked. He was a brilliant activist and civil rights attorney who was elected the mayor of Jackson, Mississippi, in 2013. His attitude was that the community should decide how to spend the money allotted to them, which I thought was so brilliant. And then, we lost him in February 2014. Not even one year after he was elected! That was a big blow to me—even before I thought about running for mayor. Losing Chokwe, to me, was a real problem for *the movement*, period. And for Black empowerment. I went through a hard time, a big depression, when we lost him. I had never met him, but I'd read about him and read some of his articles about his vision and politics. I hoped that his son, Chokwe Antar, learned a lot from his father and really absorbed his lessons. He was elected Jackson's mayor three years after his father died. Chokwe was just a brilliant man and very generous of heart.

I wanted to do something similar in Chicago to what Chokwe did. I wanted every community in Chicago's seventy-seven neighborhoods to get together and decide. Do a needs assessment. Sit in the community room with pieces of paper tacked to the walls all around the room. Have folks write down what they think they need in the community. You have to think big before you can figure things out. And then have everybody go back and prioritize. It's a very basic thing—it's not rocket science.

Here's the problem in Chicago. Chicago was designed to have a strong city council and a weak mayor—this is the way that governance was originally envisioned. But that's not what's ever *happened*. When I grew up, the original Mayor Daley—in office from 1955 to 1976—was The Mayor. As a kid, I thought you stayed mayor forever, until you didn't want to be mayor anymore. Or, like him, you just died in office. He ran the city like a kingdom. But the one thing I'll say about Mayor Old-Man Daley—he listened to what the people wanted. Now whether he *did* anything about it, this was another thing. But he would listen—because you'd hear it in his next speech or in some writing he shared or an interview or a little behind-the-scenes ordinance he might work to get passed. He had no qualms about passing out turkeys at Thanksgiving in the projects or hams at Easter. That doesn't mean he was actually doing right by Black people, but people knew who he was and, for a long time, they supported him. And the city council fell in line with whatever he wanted. They bought into—and personally benefited from—the patronage politics of the Chicago Democratic machine. The legislative branch—the city council—only rose up to assert their power when Harold Washington was elected as Chicago's first Black mayor. They used their authority *then*, but that was clearly a racist move. It wasn't because they had policy in mind.

When I got sick and it became clear I couldn't run for mayor, I endorsed Jesús "Chuy" García, then a Cook County commissioner. If I couldn't run, we still needed someone to challenge Rahm Emmanuel in the election. Chuy was a former alderman from the predominantly Mexican Little Village neighborhood who had been involved in politics and community work since the 1980s, when Harold Washington was mayor. In order to win in Chicago, you gotta bring Black and Brown together. We're already very distrustful of one another. Black people look at Brown folks like, "They took our jobs, they don't like us." And Brown folks look at Black people and say, "Y'all are just trifling, and you didn't do this, you didn't do that . . ." There's a big gap there, and you have to figure out how to fill it back up. I don't think Chuy ever grasped that. And I didn't understand why because there were people like Jitu Brown, a Black longtime organizer with the Kenwood Oakland Community Organization, who were very supportive and ready to mobilize those networks. I don't know what happened. I tried to get Chuy some help by sending him Adrienne Irmer, who I thought could maybe stir up some young Black folk for him. But Chuy had chosen people to run his campaign who just turned everybody off.

I told Chuy about it. I said, "Man, you know, the story out here on you is that you let these white dudes run everything because you think they're experts." Most minority people always look at white people and think they're the experts. They ain't shit. They don't know you, they don't know your peeps, they don't know the people you need to woo. Those white men led him astray. His campaign was a hot buttery mess. I got all kinds of phone calls around that. But, hell, I was sick! I told Chuy at one point, "Look, if I could have helped you the way you wanted me to help you, I would have run myself!" But I couldn't do it! I physically could not do it.

As I was gearing up for my campaign, I was making an effort to go to every single neighborhood in this city. It was a really good experience! I was hearing what people really wanted. And I was trying to do, in my mind, the Chokwe Lumumba piece—a real participatory democracy, which would have been revolutionary. And that's what it's gonna take in this city. It is going to take a revolution if we want to see real change. It's not gonna take incrementalism. But God had something else planned for me. So what you gonna do?

After I got sick and had to drop out of the mayor's race, I discussed my thoughts on leadership and movement building with the *Chicago Sun-Times*:

> It doesn't matter in the scheme of things, if I'm here to run something or if I'm not here to run something. The key is, what groundwork have we set? [. . .] This isn't about one election or one election cycle, it's about building a movement. And that's not going to happen overnight. We'd love for it to be, but it's not going to happen overnight. So I'm willing to work as hard as I can and give

> it my all to build the foundation and make sure we have a very strong foundation of people from all over the city that want to work together to make it better. I'm proud of the movement we built.[1]

After I suspended my campaign, people would still stop me on the street. Black people are so amazing. You know, there is *nothing* like the love of Black people. I don't know how to explain it. They don't *know* you, but they know you. They come to you with love and hugs: "Mayor Lewis!" "You should have been mayor!" I would always tell them, "God had different plans for me."

When somebody starts complaining about the mayor or politics in the city, the first thing I ask them is, "Did you vote?" If the answer is no, I tell them they can't complain. I truly believe that. And I know a lot of people who just refuse to vote because they don't like the lesser of two evils concept. I want to tell them to grow the fuck up. Because that's where we are. We have a one-party system in America, and it's the party of money—there's just two major branches, Democrats and Republicans. And if you don't believe it, look at who the donors are. Those donors will subsidize *both* branches. What we really have is one party, the party of green, and I don't mean the environmentalist green. I mean the party of *money* green. This is my theory of the situation; of course, I could be wrong as all get-out.

§

While I don't think there is a coherent Black political agenda in Chicago, I think the young people here are amazing. They're exactly what we need right now. The elders need to step out of the way and let young people come through and advocate for themselves. I love young Black organizers and I think we need to support them in any way that we can.

When the city released the horrible video of police officer Jason Van Dyke murdering seventeen-year-old Laquan McDonald in the fall of 2014, I encouraged CTU members to participate in protests to express their outrage and dignity—to turn our pain into power. Laquan McDonald had attended multiple CPS schools. In my official messaging to the CTU membership, I was clear that we stood in solidarity with all who demanded justice for his death. Instead of responding in an open and understanding way to the wave of protests that unfolded after the release of the video of Laquan's murder, the police arrested leading young activists. The criminalization of the protests was alarming.

Our message of solidarity was difficult for a lot of people who don't understand what the Black Lives Matter movement actually means. I'll be honest with you, some of my white members hated us for supporting young Black organizers. The white members that lived out in Mount Greenwood hated that I had anything to do with that.

This tension came to a head on April 1, 2016, when we held a one-day strike action. The April 1 action was for a fair contract, progressive revenue for our schools from the city and state, and for our students, parents, and communities. It was for equitable funding, good governance, and education justice. At that time, Governor Rauner seemingly was holding state funds for important public services hostage, in effect terrorizing the public. The state didn't have a budget. And the city wasn't any better, with Rahm and his latest handpicked CPS CEO, Forrest Claypool, trying to drastically cut school budgets and make teachers take a pay cut. Claypool—God, I hate him. I never hated CEOs before, but I couldn't stand him. On April 1, a week after we were forced to take a furlough day because of the mayor and governor's austerity budgeting, we joined with thousands of others, took to the streets, and marched downtown: workers in the Fight for $15 (the campaign for a living wage, collective bargaining rights, and dignity for workers), public college professors, childcare workers, health care workers, other labor unions, community organizations, and young Black Lives Matter activists. We believed it was time for us to unite to fight the mayor, the governor, and the billionaires, who were united in a Donald Trump–like campaign to turn back the hands of progress and destroy public education and our communities. My message at the rally was that we had power when we were all united against our true enemies.

Young Black organizers participated as speakers at the rally. The emcee for the rally was a teacher and CTU member who was also a member of Black Youth Project 100, a national organization of young Black activists founded in Chicago in 2013. One of several young Black organizers who spoke was Page May from Assata's Daughters, a youth-focused organizing and political education group led by young, queer Black women. At the end of her passionate speech about the many injustices facing our communities—including the murder of Laquan McDonald and other Black people by the police—she said, "Fuck the police." Afterward, she received death threats, and the Fraternal Order of Police demanded that the CTU denounce her. Some of my own white CTU members came up to me with some bullshit about apologizing for what she said. I refused. I will not diss another Black woman in public. That's just not gonna happen. Even if I don't agree with her, I'm not gonna ever do that. White folks are used to having Black people do that kind of shit, and Black people are always ready to do it.

Having the cop talk with kids sucks. When I talk to my friends with kids, I tell them what you need to do is put cops in the context of slavery and paddy rollers. If you put it in context, the police force, as it exists now, is an outgrowth of catching runaway slaves. Let's talk about the fact that they call these things paddy wagons for a reason. It should infuriate us. But it's also supposed to make us wise enough to understand that you can't argue with these people. Because they're part of a terrible institution with a racist history. And now, as Black people, we're telling our children that when somebody has a gun and a billy club and a taser, your best bet is to lay down, shut the fuck up, and put your hands over your head. That's the way you have to talk to a ten-year-old nowadays, even knowing it can't guarantee their safety.

I heard that, at a forum about public safety during her mayoral campaign in 2019, Lori Lightfoot suggested turning vacant schools into small police training academies in every community.[2] First of all, that's ridiculous. And second of all, if you're going to suggest that, you need to explain why you think that would work. I'm pretty sure I understand her thinking, that it would provide police who are sensitive to communities. But that's bullshit and gun smoke. And that is not how it works at all. They did that at a vacant school near where I live—at Price Elementary, one of the schools Rahm closed, right next to where I taught at King. They had the police canine unit being trained at the school. It was not only demoralizing to students, it was hostile. Imagine telling students, "You can't play at the new playground at the building because there are canines nearby that are being trained to attack you"?!

§

I've always wanted to help other people get to their best level for themselves, especially younger Black women. We all are responsible for doing that. I think that's important. And we have a tendency to get to the next rung and forget to bring people along with us. And I don't ever want to be that dame. I'm not her. I've had opportunities to do that, and I've tried to use them. I got to work with Stacy Davis Gates when she was our CTU political and legislative director. I think she appreciated the leadership I'd shown and the way I handled difficult situations, especially with MAGA men. And I appreciate her.

I would like to be able to advise and mentor other young Black women who have a bent toward political office or toward organizing in general, who understand the nature of politics from the ground up. Because I think that's where leadership grows. Those are the seeds of leadership. It's being able to listen, and being able to synthesize, and being able to figure that stuff out, piece by piece.

I'm trying to step back from the political thing, but I can't help myself. Because I get this stupid newspaper. Every single day they bring it to me as part of my stay at Whitehall—the rehabilitation and skilled nursing facility where I've been. Instead of calming me down, *The Chicago Tribune* makes me mad! I need a more balanced diet of papers: *South Side Weekly*, the *Chicago Reader*, and *The Chicago Defender*. I wouldn't even mind getting the *Sun-Times*, with their big, bright cover stories. So many times when I just feel like going into a deep dark spiral and start feeling sorry for myself, what I realize is I'm feeling sorry for my city. I'm feeling *so* sorry for my city. Chicago is such a great place to live—except in the winter. There are *so* many things to do here that are wonderful and amazing. To me, it's worth it. But we need to keep fighting to make our city better.

§

On October 16, 2017, I woke up at home, limped to the bathroom, and noticed that my left arm and my left leg were very weak. I told my husband, "Honey, I think I've had a stroke." John jumped out of bed and immediately called my neuro-oncologist. They told him to rush me to the emergency room. When I got to the emergency room, they were waiting for me. They put me in a CAT scan machine and started looking for a stroke. They couldn't find it, so they admitted me to the stroke floor. The doctors came the next day and told me they would have to do an MRI, but my veins were so small and squirrelly, they had a hard time inserting an IV.

Remember my brain tumor named Porky? It took them three days, but they found the stroke in my tumor bed. The radiation treatments made the blood vessels where Porky used to live febrile. The veins and arteries there were weak. So that's where my stroke happened. They sent me to the Shirley Ryan AbilityLab, what used to be called the Rehabilitation Institute of Chicago. As an inpatient, I had daily intensive therapy. Before I left Shirley Ryan, I was working on walking on a treadmill in a harness. Walking over the floor with a cane.

I had been doing fairly well at Shirley Ryan when one night, I could not stop belching and ended up throwing up. What I didn't realize at the time was that I was throwing up and defecating blood at the same time—it was coming out of both ends. I was trying to figure out what I had eaten that was black, and nothing came to mind, so I called the nurse. She freaked out and called the doctor. The doctor told me they were going to have to send me to the hospital, that there was nothing they could do for me there. When I got to the emergency department at the hospital, I was freaked out because three doctors and four nurses started working on me—an attending physician who identified himself as such and two residents. The attending was directly behind my head and the residents were to each side, so you can imagine my fear when I heard the attending bark at the nurses, "Give me two units of O positive blood, stat." As I tried to remember this detail, I asked whether O positive was the universal donor, because I am A positive. They assured me I was in good hands and would be OK. However, they still insisted on inserting a very large catheter in my neck because of my small veins.

Before they could do it, I finally had the gumption to ask, "Am I going to die tonight?" The attending said that they were trying to prevent that from happening. At that point, I decided to let them stick this giant needle in my jugular vein. One of the resident physicians said he would walk me through the whole procedure. He sat to my left and held my hand. I asked him what his name was, and he said, "John." And then I knew I was in good hands because that's my husband's name, and he takes such good care of me. I said OK. John the physician whispered in my ear, patted my hand, and said they were using an ultrasound machine to look for my jugular vein so they didn't hit anything that I'd be worried about. Thankfully, they were able to save my life.

Something similar happened when they first found Porky, my brain tumor, in 2014. When they were preparing me for surgery, I found out my neurosurgeon's name was Dr. Bloch, which is my dear friend and general counsel's name—Robert Bloch. When I had a doctor named Dr. Bloch, I knew I was in good hands. I have this great picture of me and Robert Bloch taken later, when he came to visit me. He was wearing this ignorant red-ass suit.

I said, "You went to the West Side and bought that suit, didn't you? You look like a n***a from the West Side!" It was so funny! He looked at me aghast and was like, "Karen!" And then we both laughed. I find comfort in laughter and being around the people I love.

I will never forget Dr. Bloch or John the resident, in his infinite wisdom, holding my hand and telling me that we were going to get through this together. And we did. But I can tell you that I honestly felt my life draining away from my body. I felt clammy and cold, and I thought I was going to have a seizure. When I told them I was about to have a seizure, they immediately asked for two milligrams of Ativan. Shortly after, I found myself completely relaxed and feeling that I was going to make it. I immediately thanked God in Hebrew for finding a way to save me because I wasn't ready to go, and I think we should have some say in that. I do believe people get at least a two-minute warning, and I think I had a five-minute warning. I am thankful that I haven't lost my ability to speak or to *think*. And after *two* brain surgeries *and* a stroke. Thank you, God, for letting me stay here, because my work here is unfinished.

My husband never gives up on me. John has been constantly by my side. I've been staying at Whitehall, in Deerfield, Illinois, for rehab and skilled nursing care since 2018, after Porky reared his ugly head again and I had my second brain surgery. John drives back and forth from our home on the South Side of Chicago all the way up to Deerfield, even when the weather is bad and I tell him not to. John is old school. He truly believes in "for better or worse." He says that his place is here with me. That this is where he is supposed to be.

I have a new great-grandbaby. She and John are the wallpaper on my phone. The cuteness! Her name is Michaela. To me, she looks like John. He's got some strong genes. I can't *take it* how cute she is. She's got a lot of presence. She looks like she knows something, like she's been here before. That's the way she looks to me. When I saw her picture, I was like, "I'm in love, I'm in love . . ." And every night, I kiss them both. I'm a happy camper. I *love* having grandchildren and great-grandchildren. I just think it's amazing.

And I cherish my relationship with my goddaughter, Samantha. When she was a kid, we had the most wonderful girls' days out. I'd take her to the movies, and it would just be the two of us, and her mother would always ask, "Was she good?" And I'd say, "She's always good! She's always good when she's around me! What she does at home, I don't know, but with me, she's wonderful." I loved going to her recitals. She is a singer and has a beautiful mezzo voice. And she went on to pursue her graduate degree in public policy. It's such a joy to watch young people grow up and come into their own.

§

I've enjoyed writing this. It's been cathartic, especially being honest about the cancer. And being honest to say how afraid I was. If you get scared about something, you have to figure that out. It's how you process the fear. If I've learned anything, it's that there are more cancer survivors out here than you would imagine. I recently read that one in three people will get cancer in their lifetimes. Anecdotally, I think the odds may be higher. I appreciate how people share their stories with me as if we belong to some exclusive club. I don't like being in that club—the membership dues are too high! I want to be in the spa club, where we can get massages, facials, and mani-pedis regularly. Has to be way more fun.

Despite all of these challenges, I am the ultimate optimist. I am a glass three-quarters-full kind of dame. I am *never* a Debbie Downer. That's just not who I am. I think it made me *well.*

I think it was kind of funny that I got to read my obituary. Neil Steinberg of the *Chicago Sun-Times* was updating his copy, but he mistakenly hit "publish" instead of "edit"—or he messed up something he was supposed to do. So it went online for a few minutes. I got this text from Lauren FitzPatrick, an education reporter in Chicago. It said, "Call me immediately. Call me immediately." And then I got a voicemail from Steinberg, apologizing. "Call me, call me, call me. I'm *so* sorry! I gotta tell you what I did."

I called Neil. He read the first line of it to me, which I thought was great: "Karen Lewis was fearless." I thought it was hilarious because I have all *kinds* of fears and phobias. I am one of the most claustrophobic people on the planet. When I go get an MRI, I have to have Ativan to go through that. While I think Jesse Sharkey, my VP at the CTU, who became president when I stepped down, might say that I taught him how to be fearless—you know, how to hit those mics, with the lights turned on, and be ready to answer any questions—I know I'm not fearless. But a lot of people think I am!

The loveliest thing is how often people have said to me that they know who I *am.* Which I think is interesting because they don't! They have no *clue* as to who I am really. I'm just some figure that they've seen on the TV news. But still, it's a lovely thing to be recognized as doing something good, and for people to be paying attention. I think that is awesome.

At this point in my life, it's important for me to say that I truly believe that most people try to make the best decisions they can, based on the information they have at that moment in time. But if things change, people need to reevaluate their decisions. My mother is one of those people who likes to say, "I made a decision when I was eighteen years old, and I've lived my life by it ever since." But I think life changes too much for that—I've seen a *spectacular* amount of change over the years. The thing we have to remember to do is to keep on revisiting. With new information, you can make better decisions. We *have* to keep on revisiting!

The question most people ask me is, "How did you get here?" And until I sat down to write this book, I'd never given it that much thought. I have never been a planner or a rule follower. I have always followed my heart, but with qualification: I believe in treating people with respect and kindness, unless they are disrespectful and unkind to me. Then, depending on where my spirit is at that moment, I might walk away—just cut off communication—or I might say something really snarky "when the devil kicks me in the tail," as my late sister-in-law used to say. Sometimes I'll try to make a joke, unless it's a particularly egregious offense. I really do try to keep my lips from evil, but frankly, sometimes it's really hard.

During the time I spend reflecting on my accomplishments and setbacks each year, I always find myself praying for wisdom and patience. These are tools I try to keep in my kit because they keep my mind nimble, prevent me from getting the Big Head, and help me to not be angry with people who seem to nurture petty grievances against me. I take solace in a prayer that always brings me peace:

> My God, keep my tongue from evil, my lips from lies. Help me ignore those who would slander me. Let me be humble before all. Open my heart to Your Torah.

> Frustrate the designs of those who plot evil against me; make nothing of their schemes. Act for the sake of Your compassion, Your holiness and Your Torah. Answer my prayer for the deliverance of Your People. May the words of my mouth and the meditations of my heart be acceptable to you, my Rock and my Redeemer. May the One who brings peace to His universe bring peace to us and to all the people of Israel. Amen.

There are some things that all religions seem to have in common—directives like "treat people well" or "be kind." This shows how basic and human these impulses are. It's about relationships. And this is what some people don't understand—they're so *transactional.* They don't understand that if you spend time talking to people, you can find out how much you have in common with them. When I was gearing up to run for mayor in 2014 and going all over Chicago to meet and talk with people, I felt a real connection to people living in the city. And I sensed that they felt a connection to me. A lot of it was based on the fact that I could reach out, hug them, talk to them, and treat them like they had something important to say. Because they did! I can be a good listener. All of the major religions preach this as a value.

Some people are very uncomfortable with prayer, especially sectarian prayer. Prayer gave me a whole lot of inner peace throughout my days of surgery, recovery, and treatment. People all over the world sent me well-wishes and prayers. I felt uplifted and strengthened. I have never forgotten it, and I remain grateful for the outpouring of love. It keeps me going.

LEFT: Karen's mother, Martha Gaikins Jennings, and her sisters (Karen's aunts), Nanno, Velma, Georgie, and Mary Lee

RIGHT: Karen as a baby with a football

BELOW: Kenwood High School Math and Computer Club, 1970; Karen seated in center

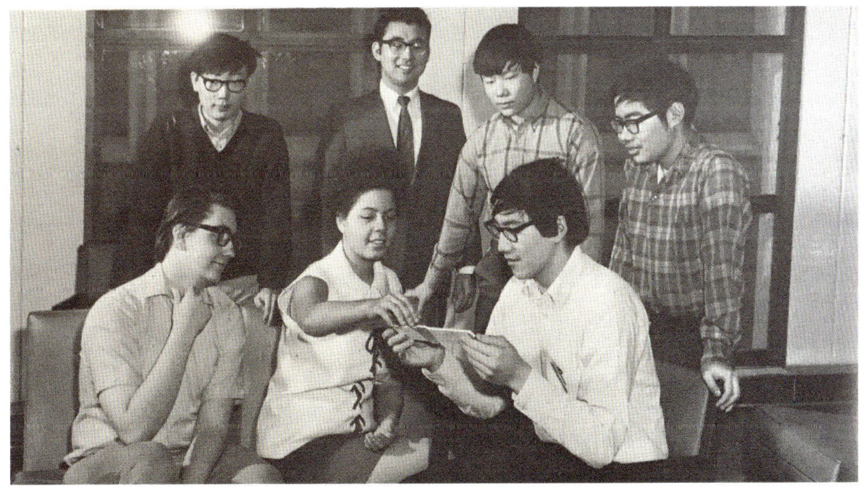

Umoja Black Student Center, Chicago, Illinois, 1968.

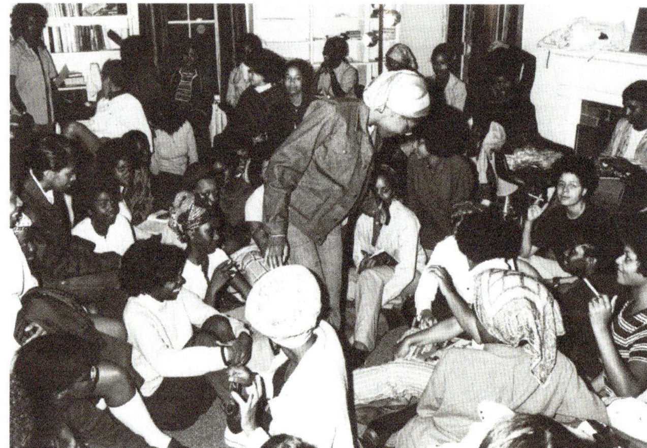

Students gathered in the Black Culture Center at Mount Holyoke College; Karen seated on far right

Karen with her mother, Martha Jennings, and grandmother, Martha Gaikins

Karen with her father, Geoffrey Jennings, and sister, Keli

Karen, seated in center, with Gaikins family relatives

Karen holding her goddaughter Samantha, 1991

Karen and John cutting their wedding cake in Hawai'i, 2001

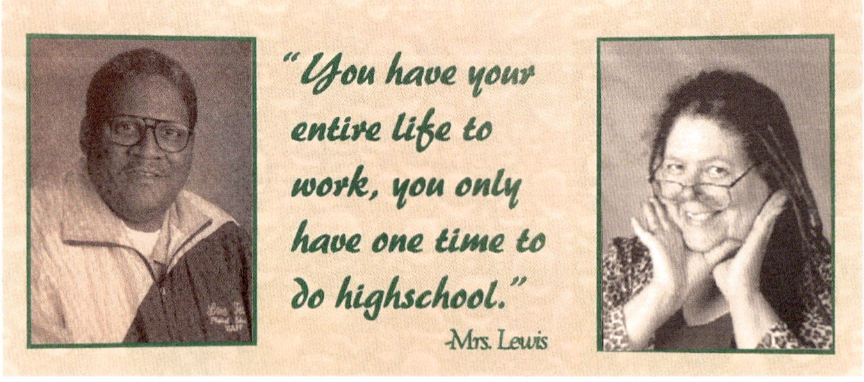

John's and Karen's Lane Tech High School yearbook pictures, 2003 and 2004

Chicago
UNION TEACHER
Volume 74 Number 1
September/October 2010

Confronting the Board In Force
page 4

www.ctunet.com

Whittier Families Take Action
Families at Whittier Dual Language School defy the wrecking ball to demand a library for their children. Page 6

The Power of Thirty Thousand
The CTU's new Organizing Department Coordinator, Norine Gutekanst, explains our strategy for rebuilding union power. Page 8

Retiree Health Care Threatened
Chicago Teachers Pension Fund Trustee James F. Ward explains the danger facing our once-solid retirement plan. Page 10

Diabetes Bill Endangers Kids
In our first "Nurse's Note" column, AFT "Everyday Hero" Lanise Sanders critiques recent health legislation. Page 15

Chicago Union Teacher, September/October 2010 cover; Michael Brunson, Jesse Sharkey, Karen, and CTU bargaining team

Karen speaking at CTU rally at the Auditorium Theatre, May 23, 2012

ABOVE: Rev. Jesse Jackson, Karen, and Congressman Bobby Rush at a rally against school closings, March 27, 2013

LEFT: Karen at her Bat Mitzvah, June 1, 2013

RIGHT: Karen receiving an honorary degree with Congressman John Lewis, 2013

ABOVE: Karen with her grandchildren Jasmine and Journey, June 2014

RIGHT: Karen marking the end of a round of cancer treatment at Northwestern University Hospital, with Dr. John Kalapurakal

LEFT: Karen on the picket line at Reavis Elementary School, April 1, 2016

Karen speaking at Fight for Funding Rally, April 1, 2016

Congresswoman Jan Schakowsky, Congresswoman Maxine Waters, American Federation of Teachers President Randi Weingarten, and Karen

Karen with Angela Y. Davis

Afterword

Stacy Davis Gates

I knew Karen was gone when I saw the name Audrey—Karen's indefatigable assistant—appear on my phone's display screen. Audrey May's voice was heavy with exhaustion and sadness and history. Her grief was compounded by the memory of burying Jackie Vaughn, the first Black woman to lead the Chicago Teachers Union. She cried for Karen and Jackie. And then she started organizing the phone tree. She gave me a list of people to inform. She gave me Jesse's list of people to inform. I was honored to be in the service of my president and I was relieved to do work and delay grieving.

Karen Lewis is the most transformative leader in Chicago in the twenty-first century. She ignited the push to create a city for the many. A chemistry teacher from the South Side of Chicago, she ignited a movement to demand, expect, and take justice on behalf of the common good. She led a movement that created more democracy for Chicagoans in a rebuke to mayoral control of Chicago Public Schools and Democratic machine politics.

Karen led the Chicago Teachers Union through one of the most tumultuous periods in Chicago history and helped the union transform into a democratic union by centering rank-and-file leadership and coalition movement building. As the pioneering leader of the Red for Ed movement, she galvanized our larger, broader movement for justice by transforming the bargaining table into a picket line for the common good—fighting not just for education justice, but also for affordable health care and housing, necessities that make sense for *everyone.* She invited the community in so our union could create contract demands that would positively impact them. Her efforts helped birth an educator-led militant labor movement anchored in the common good and racial justice. In 2012, she led thousands of teachers, paraprofessionals, and clinicians on strike for the schools Chicago's students deserve. Her leadership catalyzed a resurgence of unapologetic protest in Chicago that expanded the influence of working and progressive families in the life of the city.

Karen's unapologetic and principled leadership is as much a legacy of the Civil Rights Movement—a movement that provided her family and community with unprecedented opportunity—as it is a response to the bipartisan corporate education reform movement that targeted historically under-resourced and underfunded urban school districts and Black teachers, students, and their families. The school reform movement was and remains formidable and well funded. Former Chicago mayor Rahm Emanuel, the wealthy, irreverent, and deft hand of the Democratic Party, and right-wing political bundler and former Illinois governor Bruce Rauner were well-positioned leaders in the education reform movement. We experienced an unprecedented wave of anti-union, anti-Black, and anti–public education reforms on Chicago Public Schools and its stakeholders. It appeared Emanuel believed he had a mandate to remake Chicago's public schools without the consent of working people and Black families who worked in and attended the schools. He closed Black schools, blamed educators, fired educators, proliferated privately operated charter schools, and defunded special education, while Governor Rauner seemingly held the state budget hostage in a sustained attempt to pass a litany of unproven anti-union policies.

Karen's legendary status as leader of the most powerful union in Chicago was cemented under these unrelenting challenges. Her ability to overcome the anti-Blackness and misogyny of the city's political machinery and wealthy elite to authentically amplify the intense anger over the displacement of Black people, neglect of Black communities, and the closings of Black schools accelerated the organizing in these neighborhoods and provided people with the infrastructure to fight back. The city's political and wealthy elite wrongly assessed her leadership and the movement she led. The education reform movement mischaracterized her willingness to engage on the funding and resourcing of public education as a strategic weakness. The political establishment mocked her resistance to status quo political engagement as naive and flat. The legacy media outlets had little language and a one-dimensional understanding of movement building, and lacked the patience to learn about and engage the social justice unionism she led, so they lampooned her voice and image. Emanuel and Rauner appeared to leverage the political climate and work hand in glove to marginalize workers' rights, the Chicago Public Schools, and the public good our students and their families so desperately needed.

However, Karen understood movements and politics. She was a student of their dimensions and nuance. Her understanding, coupled with a resurgent union led by its rank and file that was anchored in a hyperdemocratic tradition, helped to shift the city's political discourse to the needs of the many and the historical disinvestment of Black and Brown neighborhoods, while finally holding the mayor of Chicago responsible for mishandling public schools. Karen, leaning into the practice of democracy, forever shifted the power dynamics in what is, perhaps, the most stubbornly segregated city and recalcitrant political machine in the world.

This was accomplished through organizing. She practiced building and sharing power with the people. She believed that common good practitioners should fight for the common good. And that Black people in Chicago deserved advocacy. Karen's leadership gave Black families—families that have survived white flight, Willis Wagons, and fifty school closings and privatization—an opportunity to shape school policy at the district level as elected members of the Chicago Board of Education.

Karen's embrace of a militant organized union anchored in the rank and file continues to shift the direction of labor nationally—from a top-down business model to a coalition of the powerful who negotiate for auto industry environmental sustainability and housing for unhoused children. Karen's commitment to leading in a democratic organization transformed teachers' unionism into the most powerful sector in labor. The 2012 CTU strike served as the proof of concept for the transformative practice of striking for bread-and-butter issues and the common good. This spawned strike actions throughout the country, in cities like Oakland and Los Angeles and states like West Virginia and Oklahoma. The bold UAW Stand Up Strikes and the unapologetic organizing and coalition building embedded in the struggles of Amazon and Starbucks worker-led organizing campaigns are direct descendants of her union's hyperemphasis on challenging labor to be a catalyst for wider social transformation.

Labor will save America. Labor has to save America. So that means that we have to stretch out to all and we have to be more courageous. Karen taught us that. There is a new generation of leaders who believe unionism is about empowering rank-and-file workers and organizing with the families that need the benefits and opportunities of a living wage and the dignity that unions provide. Unionists across industries, from baristas to warehouse workers, now fight to win better wages and equity and justice and affordable housing and migrant rights and Black liberation. Union leadership is called to a more nuanced and layered standard because of Karen's transformative leadership. Winning good contracts for workers is a component of union leadership. Now, as a result of her leadership, we are evaluated on how our contract campaigns benefit the greater societal good. Leaders are increasingly accountable to how the contract protects and expands democracy, restores our environment, wins universal and just health care, and demands racial and gender justice. Karen expanded the power and definition of a labor leader and made room for leaders like April Sims, Shawn Fain, Cecily Myart-Cruz, Chris Smalls, and Sara Nelson.

In Chicago, this style of unionism challenged the neutrality of labor's voice in popular life through building coalition movements, confronting status-quo democratic politics, creating a separate political party and a lane for progressive politics, and electing Chicago mayor Brandon Johnson, a middle-school teacher and labor organizer. His leadership is made possible through her leadership. She led with the legacy and hope and dreams of civil rights leaders, while she guided a union and its allies to redefine the public education fight in Chicago as a matter of Black liberation and left progressive coalition building in neighborhoods with community organizations. The infrastructure she helped to create made Congresswoman Delia Ramirez and Mayor Brandon Johnson inevitable. In her wake, Chicago is different, and because Chicago is different, the nation is too. The congressional "Squad" of multiracial women pushing the boundaries of the swamp speaks to the legacy of Karen Lewis.

Karen Lewis is the manifestation of her ancestors' hopes, dreams, imagination, prayers, and resilience. The brilliant daughter of Black Chicago Public School teachers. An early high school graduate from one of the most vaunted Black high schools in CPS. A member of the first coed class of graduates at Dartmouth College. A medical school dropout. A devoted wife. A film school graduate. A lover of tennis and opera. A substitute teacher. A chemistry teacher. An organizer. The most iconic labor leader of the twenty-first century. A renaissance woman.

I am, perhaps, the most direct beneficiary of Karen. I dream, speak, and behave in the unbought and unbossed chair she created for the president of the Chicago Teachers Union. She gives me the freedom to fight and win. She provides me with the space to try and fail. She never apologized for loving and leading.

Karen made this position possible for me. She left me with so much. And she's always in my ear. Karen told me to tell the truth, always tell the truth. She told the truth: in love, in jest, but in power. Karen was a curious leader who always asked: What don't I know? What am I missing? Karen said, "Ask questions, Stacy." She said, "You are your smartest, you are your best when you are engaging." Karen had doubt, insecurity, and fear, and yet she stood and led. She gave me the ability to make mistakes and the courage to use my voice. Karen was words *and* action. Karen would want us to continue to love on each other while we do this work and continue to walk in truth. Karen gets to rest in peace because she lived in power.

Notes

Introduction

1. Dan Mihalopoulos, "National Union Chief Pledges $1M if Karen Lewis Runs for Mayor," *Chicago Sun-Times*, August 19, 2014, chicago.suntimes.com/city-hall/2014/8/19/18539677/national-union-chief-pledges-1m-if-karen-lewis-runs-for-mayor.
2. The Real News Network, "Chicago Teachers Union President Karen Lewis on Fighting School Closures," YouTube Video, April 3, 2013, www.youtube.com/watch?v=HmU49BBl6Ck&t=2s; Karen Lewis, interview by Ben Bradley, "Karen Lewis 'Considering' Run for Chicago Mayor," *ABC7 News*, June 30, 2014, https://abc7chicago.com/karen-lewis-ctu-running-for-mayor-karin/148800/.

Chapter 1: There's Nothing Stopping You

1. Clinton E. Stockwell, "Englewood," *The Encyclopedia of Chicago*, http://encyclopedia.chicagohistory.org/pages/426.html.

Chapter 2: My Black Chicago Childhood

1. Arnold R. Hirsch, "Urban Renewal," *The Encyclopedia of Chicago*, http://encyclopedia.chicagohistory.org/pages/1295.html.
2. Student Racial Survey, 1968, Board of Education, Chicago Public Schools, Chicago Board of Education Archives.
3. Elizabeth Todd-Breland, *A Political Education: Black Politics and Education Reform in Chicago Since the 1960s* (Chapel Hill, NC: University of North Carolina Press, 2018).

Chapter 3: The Consciousness-Raising Years

1. Malcolm X, "The Ballot or the Bullet," speech, April 12, 1964, www.learnoutloud.com/Free-Audio-Video/History/American-History/The-Ballot-or-the-Bullet/17062.

2. Student Racial Survey, 1968, Board of Education, Chicago Public Schools, Chicago Board of Education Archives.
3. Dionne Danns, "Chicago High School Students' Movement for Quality Public Education, 1966–1971," *Journal of African American History* 88, no. 2 (2003): 138–50; and Dionee Danns, *Something Better for Our Children: Black Organizing in Chicago Public Schools, 1963–1971* (New York: Routledge, 2003).

Chapter 4: Freedom in the Happy Valley

1. Erica L. Ball, "The Politics of Pain: Representing the Violence of Slavery in American Popular Culture," in *Violence in American Popular Culture*, ed. David Schmid (Santa Barbara, CA: Praeger, 2015): 34–5.
2. Lisa Furlong, "Karen (Jennings) Lewis '74: A Chicago Teachers' Union Leader on Education Reform," *Dartmouth Alumni Magazine*, May–June 2011, https://dartmouthalumnimagazine.com/articles/karen-jennings-lewis-'74; Carol Felsenthal, "CTU President Karen Lewis: Race, Class at Center of Education Debate," *Chicago Magazine*, November 3, 2011, www.chicagomag.com/Chicago-Magazine/Felsenthal-Files/November-2011/CTU-President-Karen-Lewis-Race-Class-at-Center-of-Education-Debate/. (Author's note: Karen did not talk very much about her time at Dartmouth, and these quotes are among a few similar statements that she made in the public record. —ETB)

Chapter 6: Finding Teaching

1. Racial/Ethnic Survey-Students, 1989, Chicago Public Schools, Chicago Board of Education Archives; Racial/Ethnic Survey-Staff, 1989, Chicago Public Schools, Chicago Board of Education Archives.
2. Anthony DeBartolo, "Sullivan High Program a Lesson in Questioning," *Chicago Tribune*, April 3, 1985, www.chicagotribune.com/news/ct-xpm-1985-04-03-8501190198-story.html.

Chapter 7: Growing

1. "History," Lane Tech College Prep High School, https://lanetech.org/about/history/.
2. "History," Lane Tech College Prep; "Lane Tech HS," Chicago Public Schools, www.cps.edu/schools/schoolprofiles/lane-tech-hs.

3. "Lane Tech HS"; Dave Bartlett, "College, Junior and Community," *The Encyclopedia of Chicago*, http://www.encyclopedia.chicagohistory.org/pages/312.html.
4. Racial/Ethnic Survey-Staff, 1989; Racial/Ethnic Survey-Students, 1989; Racial/Ethnic Survey-Staff, 1991; Student Racial/Ethnic Survey, 2005; Chicago Public Schools, Chicago Board of Education Archives.

Chapter 8: My Faith

1. Clay Risen, "Lani Guinier, Legal Scholar at the Center of Controversy, Dies at 71," *New York Times*, January 7, 2022, www.nytimes.com/2022/01/07/us/politics/lani-guinier-dead.html.

Chapter 9: A Labor Awakening

1. John F. Lyons, *Teachers and Reform: Chicago Public Education, 1929–1970* (Champaign, IL: University of Illinois Press, 2008); Elizabeth Todd-Breland, *A Political Education: Black Politics and Education Reform in Chicago Since the 1960s* (Chapel Hill, NC: University of North Carolina Press, 2018).
2. LeViis Haney, "The 1995 Chicago School Reform Amendatory Act and the CPS CEO: A Historical Examination of the Administration of CEOs Paul Vallas and Arne Duncan" (PhD diss., Loyola University Chicago, 2011), https://ecommons.luc.edu/cgi/viewcontent.cgi?article=1061&context=luc_diss; Dorothy Shipps, *School Reform, Corporate Style: Chicago, 1880-2000* (University Press of Kansas, 2006); Todd-Breland, *A Political Education.*
3. Lopez v. Bridgeport Bd. of Educ., LEXIS 4379 (Conn. Super. 2013); Valerie Strauss, "Why Judge Ordered Paul Vallas Removed as Bridgeport Schools Chief," *Washington Post*, June 29, 2013, www.washingtonpost.com/news/answer-sheet/wp/2013/06/29/why-judge-ordered-paul-vallas-removed-as-bridgeport-schools-chief/; Jaclyn Zubrzycki, "Veteran Superintnedent Paul Vallas Under Fire Over Credentials," *EdWeek*, July 22, 2013, https://www.edweek.org/leadership/veteran-superintendent-paul-vallas-under-fire-over-credentials/2013/07; Jacqueline Rabe Thomas, "Judge Rules Bridgeport Superintendent Not Eligible to Run School District," *CT Mirror*, June 28, 2013, https://ctmirror.org/2013/06/28/judge-rules-bridgeport-superintendent-not-eligible-run-school-dis-

trict/; Jacqueline Rabe Thomas, "Vallas to Step Down as Leader of Bridgeport Schools," *CT Mirror*, November 8, 2013, https://ctmirror.org/2013/11/08/vallas-step-down-leader-bridgeport-schools/; Jacqueline Rabe Thomas, "Connecticut Supreme Court Dismisses Lawsuit Questioning Vallas's Qualifications," *CT Mirror*, November 14, 2013, https://ctmirror.org/2013/11/14/connecticut-supreme-court-dismisses-lawsuit-questioning-vallass-qualifications/.

Chapter 10: CTU President

1. Bill Ruthart and John Chase, "Rauner Email: Half of CPS Teachers 'Virtually Illiterate'," *Chicago Tribune*, July 22, 2016, www.chicagotribune.com/politics/ct-bruce-rauner-cps-teachers-met-0722-20160721-story.html.
2. Cassie Walker Burke, "The Rise and Fall of Juan Rangel, the Patrón of Chicago's UNO Charter Schools," *Chicago Magazine*, January 8, 2014, www.chicagomag.com/chicago-magazine/february-2014/uno-juan-rangel/; U.S. Securities and Exchange v. Juan Rafael Rangel, No. 16-6391 (N.D. Ill., 2016), https://www.sec.gov/files/litigation/complaints/2016/comp-pr2016-125.pdf; U.S. Securities and Exchange Commission, "Former CEO of Chicago Charter School Operator Settles Muni-Bond Fraud Charges," press release, June 21, 2016, https://www.sec.gov/newsroom/press-releases/2016-125; Dan Mihalopoulos, "Former UNO Boss Juan Rangel Broke Securities Law, SEC Says" *Chicago Sun-Times*, June 25, 2016, https://chicago.suntimes.com/2016/6/25/18386798/former-uno-boss-juan-rangel-broke-securities-law-sec-says.
3. Ertas Nevbahar, "Administrative Corruption and Integrity Violations in the Charter School Sector," *Public Integrity* 23, no. 1 (2021): 15–32, doi:10.1080/10999922.2020.1758535; "Another Day Another Charter Scandal," Network for Public Education, https://networkforpubliceducation.org/charter-scandals/.
4. Amanda Paulson, "New Chicago Schools Chief Has Record of Reform, but Irked Teachers," April 11, 2011, *Christian Science Monitor*, www.csmonitor.com/USA/Education/2011/0418/New-Chicago-schools-chief-has-record-of-reform-but-irked-teachers; Tiffany Lankes, "Teachers Union: No Confidence in Brizard," *Rochester Democrat and Chronicle*, February 11, 2011, https://proxy.cc.uic.edu/login?url=https://www.proquest.com/newspapers/teach-

ers-union-no-confidence-brizard/docview/851262790/se-2?accountid=14552.

5. "SB7 Goes to the Governor to Become Law," *Catalyst Chicago*, May 12, 2011, https://www.chicagoreporter.com/sb-7-goes-governor-become-law/; Howard Ryan, "Billionaires and Politicians Test Chicago Teachers Union," *Labor Notes*, May 11, 2011, https://labornotes.org/2011/05/billionaires-and-politicians-test-chicago-teachers-union; Lee Sustar, "CTU Moves to Fight Anti-Union Legislation," *Socialist Worker*, May 5, 2011, https://socialistworker.org/2011/05/05/ctu-moves-to-fight-anti-union-legislation.

Chapter 11: Strike!

1. Noreen S. Ahmed-Ullah and Tara Malone, "Chicago Public Schools Board Rescinds Teacher Raises, Angers Union," *Chicago Tribune*, June 15, 2011, www.chicagotribune.com/news/ct-xpm-2011-06-15-ct-met-cps-board-raises-0616-20110615-story.html.
2. "How to Fool the Unions and Bribe Politicians - Aspen Institute Session on SB7," posted July 10, 2011, by John Kugler, https://www.youtube.com/watch?v=ddtd0vt6oYE; George N. Schmidt, "The Union-Busting Billionaires Behind Phony 'Grass roots' Groups Like Stand For Children and Advance Illinois Have Emerged from the Shadows. . . Complete Transcript of the Remarks of Ross Wiener, James Crown and Jonah Edelman at the Aspen Institute," *Substance News*, July 12, 2011, www.substancenews.net/articles.php?page=2427.
3. Ben Goldberger, "Karen Lewis, Street Fighter," *Chicago Magazine*, October 2, 2012, www.chicagomag.com/chicago-magazine/november-2012/karen-lewis-street-fighter/; Fran Spielman, "Emanuel Calls Teachers Union Chief's Account of Private Chat 'Totally False'," *Chicago Sun-Times,* March 2, 2012, https://chicago.suntimes.com/news/2012/3/2/18533473/emanuel-calls-teachers-union-chiefs-account-of-private-chat-totally-false.
4. Rosalind Rossi, "Union Chief: Rahm 'Exploded'," *Chicago Sun-Times*, September 10, 2011, https://infoweb-newsbank-com.proxy.cc.uic.edu/apps/news/document-view?p=WORLDNEWS&docref=news/139AC80F4F5199B0; "CTU President: Enraged Mayor Swore, 'Disrespected' Her During Private Talk," *CBS 2 News*, September 9, 2011, www.cbsnews.com/chicago/news/ctu-president-

enraged-mayor-swore-disrespected-her-during-private-talk/.

5. Rossi, "Union Chief: Rahm 'Exploded'"; "CTU President: Enraged Mayor Swore, 'Disrespected' Her During Private Talk."
6. Chicago Teachers Union, *The Schools Chicago's Students Deserve: Research-based Proposals to Strengthen Elementary and Secondary Education in the Chicago Public Schools*, 2012, www.ctulocal1.org/topics/schools-students-deserve/.
7. "Chicago Teachers Union's Karen Lewis Deal Ending Strike a Victory for Education. 1 of 2," *Democracy Now!*, September 19, 2012, www.youtube.com/watch?v=vG8bGxKmV58.
8. "By the Company It Keeps: Jean-Claude Brizard," Thomas B. Fordham Institute, August 23, 2013, https://fordhaminstitute.org/national/commentary/company-it-keeps-jean-claude-brizard.
9. "Poll Reveals People Like Teachers," NBC Chicago, September 13, 2011, www.nbcchicago.com/news/local/poll-reveals-people-like-teachers/1911088/.
10. Ralph Waldo Emerson, "Circles," in *Ralph Waldo Emerson: The Major Prose*, ed. Ronald A. Bosco and Joel Myerson (Cambridge, MA: Harvard University Press, 2015), 162.
11. Lois Weiner, *The Future of Our Schools: Teachers Unions and Social Justice* (Chicago: Haymarket Books, 2012).
12. "'Mutual Agreement' Ends JC Brizard's Run as CPS CEO, NBC 5 Chicago, October 11, 2012, https://www.nbcchicago.com/news/local/chicago-public-schools-jean-claude-brizard/1942110/.
13. Illinois Department of Public Health, *2000 Census Population for Illinois, Counties, and Incorporated Areas, Illinois Center for Health Statistics*, January 2004, https://www.idph.state.il.us/pdf/2000PopulationReport.pdf; ProximityOne, "School District Population by Age and Enrollment Universe, Chicago Public School District 299, 2010," https://proximityone.com/sdst/2010/1709930.htm; Chicago Public Schools, "Racial/Ethnic Reports," www.cps.edu/about/district-data/demographics/.
14. John Chase and Noreen S. Ahmed-Ullah, "CPS Had Closings Draft Months Ago: Document Shows Mayoral Team Was Well into Planning," *Chicago Tribune*, December 19, 2012, https://www.chicagotribune.com/2012/12/19/document-shows-emanuel-administration-had-detailed-school-closing-plans-2/.
15. "Table: School Closings Over 10 Years," *The Chicago Reporter*,

December 7, 2011, www.chicagoreporter.com/table-school-closings-over-10-years/.

16. Michael Martinez, "Military Focus OKd for Carver High," *Chicago Tribune*, March 23, 2000, www.chicagotribune.com/news/ct-xpm-2000-03-23-0003230390-story.html; "Derrion Albert's Death May Be Rooted in School Closures," October 7, 2009, www.nbcchicago.com/news/local/holder-arne-duncan-fenger-city-hall-daley/1863419.
17. Josh Eidelson and Sarah Jaffe, "Defending Public Education: An Interview with Karen Lewis of the Chicago Teachers Union," *Dissent*, Summer 2013, www.dissentmagazine.org/article/defending-public-education-an-interview-with-karen-lewis-of-the-chicago-teachers-union.
18. Stephanie Farmer et al., "Challenging the Market Logic of School Choice: A Spatial Analysis of Charter School Expansion in Chicago," *Journal of Urban Affairs* 42, no. 4 (2020): 511–33; Eve L. Ewing, *Ghosts in the Schoolyard: Racism and School Closings on Chicago's South Side* (Chicago: University of Chicago Press, 2018).
19. Eidelson and Jaffe, "Defending Public Education."

Chapter 12: The Fall of the So-Called Reformers

1. Gardner, David P. et.al., "A Nation at Risk: The Imperative For Educational Reform. An Open Letter to the American People. A Report to the Nation and the Secretary of Education," 1983.
2. David Heinzmann, et al., "Emanuel-Rauner Ties Create Campaign Sub-plot," *Chicago Tribune*, August 29, 2014, www.chicagotribune.com/2014/08/29/emanuel-rauner-ties-create-campaign-subplot; Lynne Marek, "Rauner's Pension Passion," *Crain's Chicago Business*, April 6, 2013, https://www.chicagobusiness.com/article/20130406/ISSUE01/304069983/rauner-s-gtcr-long-relied-on-pension-funds-for-investment-money; Gary Rivlin, "The Private Equity Governor," *Intercept*, October 22, 2018, https://theintercept.com/2018/10/22/illinois-governor-bruce-rauner-pensions.
3. "Gov. Bruce Rauner Spent a Lot of Money on TV Advertising During the 2014 Campaign," *HuffPost*, January 30, 2015, www.huffpost.com/entry/gov-bruce-rauner-spent-a_b_6563818.
4. Bill Ruthart and John Chase, "Rauner Email: Half of CPS Teachers 'Virtually Illiterate'," *Chicago Tribune*, July 22, 2016, www.chicag-

otribune.com/politics/ct-bruce-rauner-cps-teachers-met-0722-20160721-story.html.

5. "Exclusive Details on Chicago Teachers Union Plans," *Chicago Tonight*, May 31, 2012, news.wttw.com/2012/05/31/exclusive-details-chicago-teachers-union-plans.
6. "How to Fool the Unions and Bribe Politicians - Aspen Institute Session on SB7," posted July 10, 2011, by John Kugler, https://www.youtube.com/watch?v=ddtd0vt6oYE; George N. Schmidt, "The Union-Busting Billionaires Behind Phony 'Grass roots' Groups Like Stand For Children and Advance Illinois Have Emerged from the Shadows. . . Complete Transcript of the Remarks of Ross Wiener, James Crown and Jonah Edelman at the Aspen Institute," *Substance News*, July 12, 2011, www.substancenews.net/articles.php?page=2427.
7. "Karen Lewis," *Chicago Tonight*, June 10, 2013, www.pbs.org/video/chicago-tonight-june-11-2013-karen-lewis/.
8. Carol Caref et al., *The Black and White of Education in Chicago's Public Schools: Class, Charters, and Chaos, A Hard Look at Privatization Schemes Masquerading as Public Policy*, Chicago Teachers Union, November 30, 2012, https://www.ctulocal1.org/wp-content/uploads/2018/10/CTU-black-and-white-of-chicago-education.pdf.
9. Diane Rado and Juan Perez Jr., "Chicago Is Epicenter of Charter School Teacher Contract Disputes," *Chicago Tribune*, May 26, 2017.
10. "Resolution: Calling for Moratorium on Charter School Expansion and Strengthening of Oversight in Governance and Practice," National Association for the Advancement of Colored People, 2016, https://naacp.org/resources/calling-moratorium-charter-school-expansion-and-strengthening-oversight-governance-and.
11. Carrie Spector, "School Poverty—Not Racial Composition—Limits Educational Opportunity, According to New Research at Stanford," *Stanford News*, September 23, 2019, https://news.stanford.edu/2019/09/23/new-data-tool-shows-school-poverty-leads-racial-achievement-gap/; Katherine Michelmore and Peter Rich, "Contextual Origins of Black-White Educational Disparities in the 21st Century: Evaluating Long-Term Disadvantage Across Three Domains," *Social Forces* 101, no. 4 (2023): 1918–47.
12. "Chicago Teachers Union's Karen Lewis Deal Ending Strike a Victory for Education. 2 of 2," *Democracy Now!*, September 19, 2012,

www.youtube.com/watch?v=vG8bGxKmV58&t=10s.

13. "Karen Lewis," *Chicago Tonight*.

Chapter 13: A Life Well Lived

1. "Karen Lewis, President of Chicago Teachers Union," posted January 28, 2015, by Chicago Sun-Times, www.youtube.com/watch?v=ruP0sZqXEKg.
2. Adeshina Emmanuel, "What to Do With Vacant Chicago Schools? Lightfoot Suggests Mini-Police Academies for Some," *Chalkbeat Chicago*, March 13, 2019, https://chicago.chalkbeat.org/2019/3/13/21107142/what-to-do-with-vacant-chicago-schools-lightfoot-suggests-mini-police-academies-for-some/.

Photograph Credits

Images are courtesy of John Lewis, except for the following, in order of appearance:

Kenwood High School Math and Computer Club, Kenwood Yearbook, 1970, reproduced by permission from Chicago Board of Education Archives.

Black Students Call for School Boycott, Umoja Black Student Center, Chicago, Illinois, October 14, 1968. Photo by Val Mazzenga, reproduced by permission from Chicago Tribune/TCA.

"Group of students gathered for a meeting with President David Truman in the Black Culture Center" reproduced by permission from Mount Holyoke College Archives and Special Collections.

Karen holding her goddaughter Samantha, 1991, courtesy of Ann Sarpy.

Lane Tech High School Yearbook pictures adapted from: John's 2003 yearbook picture with Karen's yearbook quote and Karen's 2004 yearbook picture. Reproduced and altered by permission from Chicago Board of Education Archives.

Chicago Union Teacher, September/October 2010 cover, courtesy of Chicago Teachers Union.

Karen speaking at CTU rally at the Auditorium Theatre, May 23, 2012 reproduced by permission from Powell Creative Services. © 2012 by Powell Creative Services.

Rev. Jesse Jackson, Karen, and Congressman Bobby Rush at March 27, 2013, rally against school closings, courtesy of Sarah-Ji @loveandstrugglephotos.

Karen on the picket line at Reavis Elementary School, April 1, 2016, courtesy of Elizabeth Todd-Breland.

Karen speaking at the Fight for Funding Rally, April 1, 2016, courtesy of Sarah-Ji @loveandstrugglephotos.

Jacket photograph of Karen Lewis © Powell Creative Services.

Jacket photograph of Elizabeth Todd-Breland by Moya Bailey.

Index

Also Available from Haymarket Books

Abolition and Social Work
Possibilities, Paradoxes, and the Practice of Community Care
Edited by Mimi E. Kim, Cameron Rasmussen, and Durrell M. Washington, foreword by Mariame Kaba

Angela Davis: An Autobiography
Angela Y. Davis

Black Lives Matter at School: An Uprising for Educational Justice
Jesse Hagopian and Denisha Jones, foreword by Opal Tometi

Care: The Highest Stage of Capitalism
Premilla Nadasen

The Future of Our Schools: Teachers Unions and Social Justice
Lois Weiner

Solidarity Is the Political Version of Love
Lessons from Jewish Anti-Zionist Organizing
Rebecca Vilkomerson and Alissa Wise
Foreword by Omar Barghouti, afterword by Stefanie Fox

Teach Truth: The Struggle for Antiracist Education
Jesse Hagopian

We Grow the World Together: Parenting Toward Abolition
Edited by Maya Schenwar and Kim Wilson

About Haymarket Books

Haymarket Books is a radical, independent, nonprofit book publisher based in Chicago. Our mission is to publish books that contribute to struggles for social and economic justice. We strive to make our books a vibrant and organic part of social movements and the education and development of a critical, engaged, and internationalist left.

We take inspiration and courage from our namesakes, the Haymarket Martyrs, who gave their lives fighting for a better world. Their 1886 struggle for the eight-hour day—which gave us May Day, the international workers' holiday—reminds workers around the world that ordinary people can organize and struggle for their own liberation. These struggles—against oppression, exploitation, environmental devastation, and war—continue today across the globe.

Since our founding in 2001, Haymarket has published more than nine hundred titles. Radically independent, we seek to drive a wedge into the risk-averse world of corporate book publishing. Our authors include Angela Y. Davis, Arundhati Roy, Keeanga-Yamahtta Taylor, Eve Ewing, Aja Monet, Mariame Kaba, Naomi Klein, Rebecca Solnit, Mohammed El-Kurd, José Olivarez, Noam Chomsky, Winona LaDuke, Robyn Maynard, Leanne Betasamosake Simpson, Howard Zinn, Mike Davis, Marc Lamont Hill, Dave Zirin, Astra Taylor, and Amy Goodman, among many other leading writers of our time. We are also the trade publishers of the acclaimed Historical Materialism Book Series.

Haymarket also manages a vibrant community organizing and event space in Chicago, Haymarket House; the popular Haymarket Books Live event series and podcast; and the annual Socialism Conference.

About the Authors

KAREN LEWIS (1953–2021) was a teacher and prominent union leader who served as the president of the Chicago Teachers Union from 2010 until 2018. Born and raised on Chicago's South Side, she was the only African American woman in her graduating class at Dartmouth College. She spent time in Oklahoma and Barbados, did stints in medical school and film school, and found spiritual grounding in Judaism later in life. Lewis ultimately discovered her passion in the classroom, where she taught high school chemistry for twenty-two years. A labor leader, an organizer, a brilliant strategist, a spirited political force, an advocate for children and public education, a symbol of the progressive left, a lover of opera, movies, and tennis, Lewis passed away in 2021.

ELIZABETH TODD-BRELAND is the author of the award-winning *A Political Education: Black Politics and Education Reform in Chicago since the 1960s* and an associate professor of history and affiliated faculty member in Black studies at the University of Illinois Chicago. She is a scholar of twentieth-century US urban and social history, African American history, the history of education, and education policy. Todd-Breland served as a member of the Chicago Board of Education from 2019 until 2024.